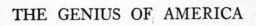

THE GENIUS OF AMERICA

THE GENIUS OF AMERICA

STUDIES IN BEHALF OF THE YOUNGER GENERATION

BY
STUART P. SHERMAN

AUTHOR OF " AMERICANS," " ON CONTEMPORARY LITERATURE," ETC.

Keep the young generations in hail,
And bequeath them no tumbled house.

CHARLES SCRIBNER'S SONS
NEW YORK · LONDON
1931

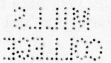

PREFACE

It was, I believe, no less an authority than Napoleon who declared that there is no indispensable man. This remark has always seemed to me to strike more deeply into the truth of human affairs than Carlyle's saying that history is the biography of great men. Consequently, I was a little surprised after the appearance of my recent book, *Americans*, to find one of my most intelligent reviewers classifying me as a "hero-worshipper." Great men serve the explorer of a nation's genius as eminent peaks in a mountain range serve the geologist whose eye, travelling swiftly from peak to peak, sees at a glance what course that vast power has taken which has crumpled a continent. But the hero of my book is neither Emerson nor Roosevelt, by including whom among Americans I have, according to one candid correspondent, written my "obituary."

My hero is that continuous power of the national life in the existence of which all our great

men appear but as momentary eddies and transient formations in the current. They have
achieved greatness only in proportion to their
capacity to receive this streaming energy. The
most useful pursuit of our history and biography
must always lead us from the study of forms to
the study of the formative spirit, from the study
of individuals to the study of that creative force
of which they are but temporary representatives. Where does it reside—in what institutions, in what customary and traditional beliefs,
in what elements of the popular culture—that
genius of America which dispenses, one after
another, with all its great servants, and confidently entrusts the destiny of a people to un-
tried hands?

In this book, which is a kind of sequel to
Americans, I have made some rudimentary attempts at an answer. Two of the essays here
appear for the first time in print: "Vocation"
and "Literature and the Government of Men."
For permission to reprint the others I am in-
debted as follows: to *The Atlantic Monthly* for
"The Genius of America," "What Is a Puritan?" and "The Point of View in American
Criticism"; to *The Nation* for "A Conversation

on Ostriches" and "Education by the People";
to *McCall's Magazine* for "The Shifting Centre
of Morality"; and to *The Literary Review* for
"The Superior Class."

S. P. S.

CONTENTS

I

THE GENIUS OF AMERICA

It is a secret which every intellectual man quickly learns, that, beyond the energy of his possessed and conscious intellect, he is capable of a new energy (as of an intellect doubled on itself), by abandonment to the nature of things; that, beside his privacy of power as an individual man, there is a great public power, on which he can draw, by unlocking, at all risks, his human doors, and suffering the ethereal tides to roll and circulate through him.

EMERSON.

If you have built castles in the air your work need not be lost; that is where they should be. Now put the foundations under them.

THOREAU.

*I said to my silent, curious Soul, out of the bed of the
    slumber-chamber
Come, for I have found the clue I sought so long,
Let us go forth refresh'd amid the day,
Cheerfully tallying life, walking the world, the real,
Nourish'd henceforth by our celestial dream.*

WHITMAN.

His hobby had turned into a camel, and he hoped, if he rode long enough in silence, that at last he might come on a city of thought along the great highways of exchange.

HENRY ADAMS.

When you get old enough, you'll wake up some day with the feeling that the world is much more beautiful than it was when you were young, that a landscape has a closer meaning, that the sky is more companionable, that outdoor colour and motion are more splendidly audacious and beautifully rhythmical than you had ever thought. That is true.

WALTER HINES PAGE.

THE GENIUS OF AMERICA

Some people have one hobby and some another. Mine is studying the utterances of the Intelligentsia—a word by which those who think that they exhibit the latest aspect of mind designate themselves. I like to hear what our "young people" say, and to read what they write; for, though they are not meek, they will, at least in a temporal sense, inherit the earth—and one is always interested in heirs. So much depends upon them.

Not long ago, progressive thinkers organized a public dinner in order to consult together for the welfare of the Republic. The marks of a progressive thinker are profound pessimism with regard to the past and infinite hope with regard to the future. Such a thinker was the toastmaster. Now, a thoughtful and progressive pessimist is a joy forever. He says for the rest of us those bitter things about history and society which we all feel at times, but hesitate to utter, not being so certain that we possess the antidote. I had long surmised that this was not the best possible of worlds, whether one considered it in its present drunken and reeling state, or whether one peered backward, through stratum after stratum of wrecked enterprises, into its iniquitous and catastrophic antiquity. Accordingly, I felt a kind of rich, tragic satisfaction when this toastmaster, in a ten-minute introduction, reviewed the entire history of the world from the time of the Cave Man to the time of the Treaty of Versailles, and concluded with a delightfully cheerful smile:—

"Up to date civilization has been a failure. Life is tolerable only as a preparation for a state which neither we nor our sons shall enter. We shall all die in the desert," he continued, as the gloom thickened to emit the perorational flash; "but let us die like Moses, with a look into the Promised Land."

Then he began to call upon his associates in the organization of progress.

Nine-tenths of the speakers were, as is customary on such occasions, of the sort that editors include when they arrange a series of articles called "Builders of Contemporary Civilization." They were the men who get cathedrals begun, and make universities expand, legislatures vote, armies fight, money circulate, commodities exchange, and grass grow two blades for one.

They spoke in a businesslike way of eliminating waste and introducing efficiency, of tapping unused resources here, of speeding up production there, of facilitating communications somewhere else. Except for the speeches of the bishop and the university president, the discourses had to my ear a somewhat mechanical twang. Yet one could not but approve and feel braced by the leading idea running through them all, which was to extend the control of man over nature and the control of a creative reason over man. All the speakers—engineer, banker, and farmer, no less than clergyman and educator—seemed to have their eyes fixed on some standard, which some internal passion for improvement urged them to approximate, or to attain. I couldn't help thinking how Franklin would have applauded the spirit of his posterity.

When, as I thought, the programme was completed, they had substituted for the present machinery of society a new outfit of the 1950 model, or perhaps of a still later date. The country, under intensive cultivation, looked like a Chinese garden. The roads, even in the spring of the year, were not merely navigable but Fordable. Something had happened to the great smoke-producing cities; so that Chicago, for instance, shone like a jewel in clear air and sunlight. High in the heavens, innumerable merchant vessels, guarded by aerial dreadnaughts, were passing in continuous flight across the Gulf to South America. Production had been so enormously increased by the increased expertness, health, and sobriety of the producers, that a man could go to market with only a handful of silver in his pocket and return with bread and butter enough for himself and his wife, and perhaps a couple of biscuits for his dog. Every one of the teeming population, alow and aloft, male and female, was at work in uniform, a rifle and a wireless field-telephone within easy reach; for every one was both an expert workman and a soldier. But no one was fighting. Under the shield of that profound "preparedness," the land enjoyed uninterrupted peace and prosperity.

Perhaps I dreamed some of this. The speeches were long.

When I returned to a condition of critical consciousness, the toastmaster was introducing the last speaker as follows: "We have now provided for all matters of first-rate importance. But we have with us one of the literary leaders of the younger generation. I am going to call upon him to say a word for the way the man of the new Republic will express himself after he has been fed and clothed and housed. I shall ask him to sketch a place in our programme of democratic progress for art, music, literature, and the like—in short, for the superfluous things."

That phrase, "The superfluous things," rang in my ear like a gong: not because it was new, but because it was old; because it struck a nerve sensitive from repeated striking; because it really summed up the values of art for this representative group of builders; because it linked itself up with a series of popularly contrasted terms—practical and liberal studies, business English and literary English, useful and ornamental arts, valuable and graceful accomplishments, necessaries and luxuries of life, chemists and professors of English, and so on *ad infinitum*. I myself was a professor of superfluous things, and therefore, a superfluous professor. As I turned this uncomfortable thought over in my mind, it occurred to me that things are superfluous only with reference to particular ends; and that, in a comprehensive plan of preparation for a satisfactory national life, we might be compelled to revise the epithets conventionally applied to the arts which express our craving for beauty, harmony, happiness.

Before I had gone far in this train of thought, the literary artist was addressing the business men. His discourse was so remarkable, and yet so representative of our most conspicuous group of "young people," that I reproduce the substance of it here.

"The young men of my generation," he began, "propose the emancipation of the arts in America. Before our time, such third-rate talents as the country produced were infected, by our institutions, and by the multitude, with a sense of their Messianic mission. Dominated by the twin incubi of Puritanism and Democracy, they servilely associated themselves with political, moral, and social programmes, and made beauty a prostitute to utility. Our generation of artists has seen through all the solemn humbug of your plans for the "welfare of the Republic." With a clearer-eyed pessimism than that of our toastmaster, we have not merely envisaged the failure of civilization in the past: we have also foreseen its failure in the future.

"We have talked with wiser counselors than those pious Philistines, our naïve Revolutionary Fathers. George Moore, our great contemporary, tells us that 'Humanity is a pig-sty, where liars, hypocrites, and the obscene in spirit congregate: and it has been so since the great Jew conceived it, and it will be so till the end.' Leopardi, who in this respect was our pioneer, declares that 'all things else being vain, disgust of life represents all that is substantial and real in the life of man.' Theodore Dreiser, our profound philosophical novelist, views the matter, however, with a bit of creative hopefulness. Though God, as he has assured us, cares nothing for the pure in heart, yet God does offer a 'universe-eating career to the giant,' recking not how the life-force manifests itself, 'so long as it achieves avid, forceful, artistic expression.' From serving the middle-class American, Flaubert frees us, saying, 'Hatred of the bourgeois is the beginning of virtue.' Mr. Spingarn, our learned theorist, brushes away the critical cobwebs of antique poetic doctrine, and gives us a clean æsthetic basis, by his revelation that 'beauty aims neither at morals nor at truth'; and that 'it is not the purpose of poetry to further the cause of democracy, or any other practical "cause," any more than it is the purpose of bridge-building to further the cause of Esperanto.' We have had to import our philosophy in fragments from beyond the borders of Anglo-Saxonia, from Ireland, Germany, France, and Italy; and we have had to call in the quick Semitic intelligence to piece it together. But here it is; and you will recognize that it liberates us from Puritanism and from Democracy. It emancipates us from you!

'You ask me, perhaps,' continued the young representative of American letters, 'what we intend to do with this new freedom, which, as Mr. Ludwig Lewisohn truly says, is our "central passion." Well, we intend *to let ourselves out.* If you press me as to what I mean by that, I can refer you to the new psychology. This invaluable science, developed by great German investigators, has recently announced, as you possibly know, an epoch-making discovery— namely, that most of the evil in the world is due to self-control. To modern inquiry, it appears that what all the moralists, especially in Anglo-Saxon countries, have tried to curb or to suppress is precisely what they should have striven to release. If you wish corroboration, let me quote the words of our talented English colleague, Mr. W. L. George, the novelist, who says, "I suspect that it does a people no good if its preoccupations find no outlet."

" 'In passing I will remark that Mr. George, being an Englishman, shows a certain taint of inherited English Puritanism in defending letting the people out *in order to do them good.* From the point of view of the new philosophy,

letting one's self out completely and perfectly
is art, which has no purpose and therefore
requires no defense.

'But to return: what are the "preoccupations"
of the ordinary man?   Once more Mr. George
shall answer for us.   "A large proportion of his
thoughts run on sex if he is a live man."   French
literature proves the point abundantly; American literature, as yet, very imperfectly and
scantily.   Consequently, a young American
desiring to enlarge his sex-consciousness must
import his fiction from overseas.   But our own
Mr. Cabell has also begun to prove the point
as well as a foreigner.   His release of the suppressed life is very precious.   If he were
encouraged, instead of being nipped by the frost
of a Puritanical censorship; if a taste were
developed to support him, he might do for us
what George Moore is trying, subterraneously,
to do for England.

'Our own Mr. Dreiser has been so preoc-
cupied with this subject that he has been
obliged to neglect a little his logic and his
grammar.   His thinking, however, runs none
the less surefootedly to the conclusion reached
by Mr. George.   What does that remorseless
artist-thinker, Mr. Dreiser, say?   He says:
"It is the desire to enthrone and enhance, by

every possible detail of ornamentation, comfort, and color,—love, sensual gratification,—that man in the main moves, and by that alone." We do not maintain that Mr. Dreiser is a flawless writer. But if, at your leisure, you will study that sentence from his latest and ripest book, till you discover its subject, predicate, and object, and can bridge its anacoluthon, and reconcile "in the main" with "by that alone," then you will be in a position to grasp our leading idea for the future of the arts in America.'

When the young man resumed his seat, there was a ripple of applause among the ladies, one of whom told me later that she thought the speaker's voice 'delicious' and his eyes 'soulful.' But I noticed that the bishop was purple with suppressed wrath; that the university president had withdrawn; while the other builders of civilization, notably the business men, were nodding with a kind of patient and puzzled resignation.

In my neighborhood there was a quick little buzz of questions: 'Will you tell me what all that has to do with a programme of democratic progress?'—'What is George Moore trying subterraneously to do for England? Is he interested in the collieries? I thought he was a novelist.'—'He has downright insulted them,' said my neighbor on the right, 'don't you think?'

'Why, no,' I replied, 'not exactly. He was asked to speak on the superfluous things; and he has really demonstrated that they are superfluous. After this, don't you see, the builders of civilization can go on with their work and not worry about the arts. He has told them that beauty is not for them; and they will swiftly conclude that they are not for beauty. I think he has very honestly expressed what our radical young people are thinking. They are in revolt. They wish by all means to widen the traditional breach between the artist and the Puritan.'

'What do you mean by Puritan?' inquired my friend, as we made our way out of the hall together.

He is a simple-hearted old gentleman who doesn't follow the new literature, but still reads Hawthorne and George Eliot.

'It is n't,' I explained, 'what I mean by Puritan that signifies. It is what the young people mean. A Puritan for them is any man who believes it possible to distinguish between good and evil, and who also believes that, having made the distinction, his welfare depends upon his furthering the one and curbing the other.'

'But,' cried the old gentleman in some heat,

'in that sense, we are all Puritans. That is n't theological Puritanism. That is scarcely even moral Puritanism. It's just—it's just ordinary horse sense. In that sense, for God's sake, who is n't a Puritan?'

I recalled an old case that I thought would illustrate the present situation. 'There was Judge Keeling,' I said, 'in Charles the Second's time. Judge Keeling put Bunyan in jail for failing to use the Book of Common Prayer, and similar misdemeanors. In the reign of the same Defender of the Faith, two merry wits and poets of his court became flown with wine and, stripping themselves naked, ran through the streets, giving a healthy outlet to their suppressed selves in songs of a certain sort. The constable, an ordinary English Puritan, so far misunderstood the spiritual autonomy which the artist should enjoy, that he arrested the two liberators of art. When, however, the news reached Judge Keeling, he released the young men and laid the constable by the heels; which, as Pepys,—himself a patron of the arts, yet a bit of a Puritan,—as Pepys remarked, was a "horrid shame." Now Judge Keeling, I think our own young people would admit, was not a Puritan, even in the latest sense of the term.'

'But those Restoration fellows,' replied my

friend,—'Keeling and the wits and the rest of them,—they were opposing the sense of the whole English nation. They made no headway. No one took them seriously. They all disappeared like gnats in a snowstorm. When the central current of English life had done its scouring work, people thought of your two poets as mere stable-boys of the Restoration. Surely you don't think our democratic young people are so silly as to imitate them? We have no merry monarch to reward them. What do they gain by setting themselves against the common sense?'

'Notoriety,' I said, 'which is as sweet under a republican as under a monarchical form of government. I used to think that to insult the common sense and always to be speaking contemptuously of the "bourgeoisie," implied sycophancy, either to a corrupt and degenerate aristocracy, or to a peculiarly arrogant and atheistical lowest class. But our "democratic young people," as you call them, preserve and foster this artistic snobbishness as a form of self-expression.

'When Mr. Dreiser declares that God cares nothing for the Ten Commandments or for the pure in heart, he really means that inanimate nature cares nothing for them, and that the animal kingdom and he and the heroes of his books follow nature. But he denies a faith which in some fifty millions of native Americans survives the decay of dogma, and somehow in attenuated form, keeps the country from going wholly to the dogs. For, of course, if it were demonstrable that God had abandoned a charge so important, plain men of sense would quietly assume responsibility and "carry on" in his stead.'

'I quite agree with you,' said the old gentleman; 'but as I am not acquainted with the author you mention and am just completing my third reading of *Middlemarch,* I will turn in here. Good-night.'

I went on down the street, resuming, unaccompanied, the more difficult part of my meditation on the place of the fine arts in a programme of democratic progress, and internally debating with the young man who had caused such a sensation at dinner. Having made this general acknowledgment of his inspiration, I shall not attempt to reproduce our dialogue; for I found that he simply repeated the main points of his speech, and interrupted my comment upon it.

When Mr. Spingarn, who, as a man, is concerned with truth, morals, and democracy, and has a personal record of civil and military service — when Mr. Spingarn, as an aesthetic theorist, declares that beauty is not concerned with truth or morals or democracy, he makes a philosophical distinction which I have no doubt that Charles the Second would have understood, approved, and could, at need, have illustrated.   But he says what the American schoolboy knows to be false to the history of beauty in this country.   By divorcing, in his super-subtle Italian fashion, form from substance, he has separated beauty from her traditional associates in American letters, and so has left her open to seduction.

Beauty, whether we like it or not, has a heart full of service.   Emancipated, she will still be seeking some vital activity.   You have heard how the new writers propose to employ her new leisure: in extending the ordinary man's preoccupation with sex.   We don't, you will observe, by the emancipation of the arts from service to truth, morals, and democracy—we don't obtain a 'disinterested' beauty.   We obtain merely a beauty with different interests—serving 'sensual gratification' and propagating the curiously related doctrine that God cares nothing for the Ten Commandments or for the pure in heart.

We arrive finally at some such comprehensive formulation of relationships as this: It is the main function of art to deny what it is the main function of truth, morals, and democracy to affirm. Our speaker for the younger generation has made all this so clear that I suspect the bishop is going home resolved to take music out of his churches. The university president is perhaps deciding to replace his professor of Italian painting by an additional professor of ooil fertility. As for the captains of industry, they can hardly be blamed if they mutter among themselves: 'May the devil fly away with the fine arts! Let's get back to business.'

It is to be hoped, nevertheless, that the devil will not fly away with the fine arts or the fine artists, or with our freshly foot-loose and wandering beauty; for the builders of civilization have need of them. If the young people were not misled by more or less alien-spirited guides, the national genius itself would lead them into a larger life.

When our forefathers, whom it is now customary to speak of as 'grim,' outlined their programme for a new republic, though they had many more immediately pressing matters on their minds, they included among objects to be safeguarded, indeed, among the inalienable

rights of mankind, 'the pursuit of happiness.'
It appears that they, like ourselves, had some
dim idea that the ultimate end of their preparation was, not to fight the English or the savages
or the wilderness, but to enjoy, they or their
posterity, some hitherto unexperienced felicity.
That, at heart, was what sustained them under
the burdens and heats of a pioneering civilization, through those years when they dispensed
with such ingredients of happiness as musical
comedy and moving pictures, and when the
most notable piece of imagist verse was Franklin's proverb, 'It is hard for an empty sack to
stand upright'—a one-line poem of humor,
morality, insight, and imagination all compact.

We, too, entertain, we ordinary puritanical
Americans, some shadowy notions of a time,
when, at more frequent intervals than now, men
shall draw in a delighted breath and cry, 'Oh,
that this moment might endure forever!' We
believe in this far-off time, because, at least once
or twice in a lifetime, each of us experiences
such a moment, or, feeling the wind of its
retreating wing, knows that it has just gone by.
It may have been in the spell-bound glow of
some magical sunset, or at the sound of a
solemn music, or in the sudden apprehension of a long-sought truth, or at the

thrill and tightening of resolution in some crisis, or in the presence of some fair marble image of a thought that keeps its beauty and serenity while we fret and fade. It may even have been at some vision, seen in the multitude of business, of a new republic revealed to the traveling imagination, like a shining city set on a hill in the flash of a midnight storm. Till life itself yields such moments less charily, it is incumbent upon the artist to send them as often as he can.

There came among us in war time an English poet whose face was as sad as his who from the Judecca climbed to see again *delle cose belle che porta il ciel*—the sky-borne beauty of the stars. He had been where his countrymen, fighting with incredible heroism, had suffered one of the most heart-breaking and bloody defeats in English history. His memory was seared with remembrance of the filth, waste, wounds, and screaming lunacy of the battle-front to which he was about to return. When someone asked him to write his name in a volume of his poems, he inscribed below it this line of his own verse:—

The days that make us happy make us wise.

Why these days? Because in them we learn the final object of all our preparation. These days serve us as measures of the success of our civilization.

The ultimate reason for including the 'superfluous things'—art, music, literature—in a plan of national preparation is that, rightly used, they are both causes and consequences of happiness. They are the seed and the fruit of that fine and gracious and finished national life towards which we aspire. When the body is fed and sheltered, there remain to be satisfied—as what Puritan does not know?—the inarticulate hungers of the heart, to which all the arts are merely some of the ministers. Other ministers are religion, morality, patriotism, science, truth. It is only by harmonious coöperation that they can ever hope to satisfy the whole heart, the modern heart, with its ever-widening range of wakened hungers. It is certainly not by banishing or ignoring the austerer ministers, and making poetry, painting, and music perform a Franco-Turkish dance of sensual invitation—it is not thus that the artist should expect to satisfy a heart as religious, as moral, and as democratic as the American heart is, by its bitterest critics, declared to be.

'Art is expression,' says the learned theorist of the young people, 'and poets succeed or fail by their success or failure in completely expressing themselves.' Let us concede that the poet who expresses completely what is in him by a hymn to the devil is as perfect an artist as a poet who expresses what is in him by the Iliad. Then let us remark that the poet who hymns the devil, the devil is likely to fly away with. And let us add as rapidly as possible a little series of neglected truisms. An artist is a man living in society. A great artist is a great man living in a great society. When a great artist expresses himself completely, it is found invariably that he has expressed, not merely himself, but also the dominant thought and feeling of the men with whom he lives. Mr. Spingarn, indeed, indirectly admits the point when he says: 'If the ideals they [the poets] express are not the ideals we admire most, we must blame, not the poets, but ourselves; in the world where morals count, *we have failed to give them the proper materials out of which to rear a nobler edifice.*' (Italics mine.) This seems to mean that society is responsible for the artist, even if the artist is not responsible to society. Society gives him, as a man, what, as an artist, he expresses.

I have perhaps hinted here and elsewhere my suspicion that Mr. Dreiser, a capital illustrative example, is not a great novelist, because, though living in a great society, he does not express or represent its human characteristics, but confines himself to an exhibition of the habits and traits of animals. Is it that we have not given him materials to rear a nobler edifice? That which we—that is, society—can give to a novelist is the moulding and formative influence of the national temper and character. What have we given to Mr. Dreiser? What, in short, are the dominant traits of the national genius? I am delighted to discover in Mr. Dreiser's latest book that he himself knows pretty well what the national genius is, how it has manifested itself in religion and politics, and how it is nourished and sustained by ancient traditions and strong racial proclivities. I like to agree with our young people when I can. When I find one of them testifying, contrary to their custom, that America does now possess a powerful national culture, I like to applaud his discernment. It is a pleasure to make amends for my disparagement of Mr. Dreiser as a novelist, by illustrating his critical ability with these words of his on the national genius:—

'No country in the world (at least, none that I know anything about) has such a peculiar, such a seemingly fierce determination to make the Ten Commandments work. It would be amusing, if it were not pitiful, their faith in these binding religious ideals. I have never been able to make up my mind whether this springs from the zealotry of the Puritans who landed at Plymouth Rock, or whether it is rooted in the soil . . . or whether it is a product of the Federal Constitution, compounded by such idealists as Paine and Jefferson and Franklin and the more or less religious and political dreamers of the preconstitutional days. *Certain it is that no such profound moral idealism animated the French in Canada, the Dutch in New York, the Swedes in New Jersey, or the mixed French and English in the extreme South and New Orleans.'* (Italics mine.)

I know how differently our young people feel; but, to my thinking, a national genius animated by an incomparably profound moral idealism does not seem such a contemptible moulding and formative influence for an artist to undergo. English-speaking poets, from Spenser to Walt Whitman, have grown great under the influence of such an environing spirit. At any rate, if the great artist, in expressing himself, expresses also the society of which he is a part, it should seem to follow, like a conclusion in geometry, that a great American artist must express the 'profound moral idealism' of America. To rail against it, to lead an insurrection against it, is to repeat the folly of the Restoration wits. If in this connection one may use a bit of the American language, it is to 'buck' the national genius; and this is an enterprise comparable with bucking a stone wall. On the other hand to acknowledge the leadership of the national genius, to subject one's self to its influence, to serve it according to one's talents, to find beautiful and potent forms to express its working—this is to ally one's self with the general creative effort of the country in all fields of activity; this is to be in a benign conspiracy with one's time and place, and to be upborne by the central stream of tendency.

There is small place for Bohemia in democratic art. I sometimes wonder with what spiritual refugees, under what rafters, those poets and novelists live who are so anxious to secede from the major effort of their countrymen. For their own sakes one wishes that they might cultivate acquaintance with our eminent 'builders of civilization.' The good that I should expect from this contact is a vision of the national life, a sense of the national will, which are usually possessed in some degree by those Americans, whatever their æsthetic deficiencies, who bear the burden of the state, or are widely conversant with its business, or preside over its religious, moral, or educational undertakings. I do not intend in the least to suggest that the artist should become propagandist or reformer, or that he should go to the bishop or the statesman for a commission, though I believe that Leonardo and Michael Angelo did some very tolerable things under direct inspiration of that nature. What one feels is rather that intercourse with such men might finally create in our artistic secessionists a consciousness of the ignobility of their aims. For in America it will be found more and more that the artist who does not in some fashion concern himself with truth, morals, and democracy, is unimportant, is ignoble.

In an unfinished world, where religion has become so largely a matter of traditional sentiments and observances, poetry has a work to do, poetry of any high seriousness. Our critics and poets of vision have long since recognized what that work is. 'I said to Bryant and to these young people,' wrote Emerson in his journal many years ago, 'that the high poetry of the world from the beginning has been ethical, and it is the tendency of the ripe modern mind to produce it.' — 'I hate literature,' said Whitman, perhaps over-emphatically expressing the tra-

ditional American disdain for art in its merely
decorative and recreative aspects. 'Literature
is big only in one way, when used as an aid in
the growth of the humanities.' Our young people, of course, will exclaim that these are typical
utterances of our New England Puritanism,
fatal to the arts; but, as a matter of fact, this
Puritanism is of a sort that the New Englanders
shared with Plato and Aristotle, who have not
been fatal to the arts. When Emerson said,
'Honor every truth by use,' he expressed, I
think, what Socrates would have approved, and
at the same time he spoke in fullest accord with
the national genius, ever driving at practice,
ever pressing towards the fulfillment of its
vision.

Why should a spokesman for *belles-lettres,*
bred in the national tradition, hesitate to go
before a group of 'practical' men and talk to
them, unashamed, of the 'utilities' of artistic
expression? He may borrow a figure from the
economist, and declare that the poet 'socializes'
the spiritual wealth of the country. Art is
rooted in social instinct, in a desire to communicate goods to others, to share one's private
experience and anticipations. It is the spontaneous overflow of thoughts and feelings which
one cannot consume alone. 'Full of the com-

mon joy,' says Donne, 'I uttered some.' This is your true and unassailable communism. When Saint Gaudens, having conceived his heroic and inspiring image of Colonel Shaw leading his colored troops, sets it up on Boston Common, it becomes common property; and the loafer in the park, the student, the hurrying merchant, the newsboy, are equal sharers in its commemoration and inspiration. A village poet with an ethical bent makes this thought sing :—

> When duty whispers low, 'Thou must,'
> The youth replies, 'I can,'—

and he has slipped a spiritual gold-piece into the palm of each of his fellow countrymen. This is wealth really distributed. It would be of advantage to both bards and business men if some spiritual economist would remind them more frequently that the wealth of a community is in proportion to the number of such ideas that it has in common.

Among builders of American civilization, many means are now discussed for awakening national pride and attaching the affections of the people to the state; conspicuous among them are, or were, Liberty Bonds, nationalization of the railroads, and universal military service.

Robert Burns and Sir Walter did the work more simply and cheaply for Scotland. It has never been hard for the native-born American to hold America 'first' in political affairs; but musicians as such, painters as such, men of letters as such, cannot, without straining the meaning of the word, hold her first till her national genius expresses itself as adequately, as nobly, in music, painting, and literature, as it has, on the whole, in the great political crises. Irving, at the beginning of the last century, worked with a clear understanding of our deficiencies when he wrote his *Rip Van Winkle* and other legends of the Hudson Valley, with the avowed purpose 'to clothe home scenes and places and familiar names with those imaginative and whimsical associations so seldom met with in our new country, but which live like charms and spells about the cities of the Old World, binding the heart of the native inhabitant to his home.'

You may persuade all men to buy Liberty Bonds or to invest in the stock of nationalized railroads, or you may legislate them into the army; but you cannot dragoon them into crying, 'O beautiful, my country!' That is the work of the poets, who have entwined their loyalty with their heart-strings. That is the work of the artists, who have made their Ameri-

canism vital, devout, affectionate. 'How can
our love increase,' asks Thoreau, 'unless our
loveliness increases also?'   A good question for
'Americanizers' to meditate upon.   It would
benefit both public men and artists if someone
reminded them more frequently that one of the
really important tasks of national preparation
is to draw out and express in forms of appealing
beauty, audible as poetry or music, visible as
painting or sculpture, the purpose and meaning
of this vast half-articulate land, so that our hosts
of new and unlearned citizens may come to
understand her as they understand the divine
compassion—by often kneeling before some
shrine of the Virgin.

When art becomes thus informed with the
larger life of the country, it vitalizes and gives
permanency to the national ideals.   It trans-
mits the hope and courage and aspiration of one
generation to the next, with the emotional glow
and color undiminished and unimpaired.   If
we receive and cherish the tradition, our imaginative experience transcends the span of our
natural lives.   We live in the presence, as Burke
declared, of our 'canonized' forefathers and in
a kind of reverent apprehension of our posterity,
happily conscious of a noble and distinguished

national thought and feeling, 'above the vulgar practice of the hour.'

Precisely because Lincoln had communed intimately with the national genius and obeyed devoutly its promptings, America ceases, in some passages of his letters and speeches, to be a body politic and·becomes a living soul. Who was it wrote that letter to Mrs. Bixby on the loss of her five sons in battle? 'I cannot refrain from tendering to you the consolation that may be found in the thanks of the Republic that they died to save. I pray that our Heavenly Father may assuage the anguish of your bereavement, and leave you only the cherished memory of the loved and lost, and the solemn pride that must be yours to have laid so costly a sacrifice upon the altar of freedom.'

The words are thrilling still with the pathos and splendor of patriotic death. They seem charged with the tears and valor of the whole Civil War. To speak like that of death is to unfold the meaning of the Latin verse: *Dulce et decorum est pro patria mori*. It is to hallow the altar on which the sacrifice is made. One can hardly read the letter through with dry eyes; and yet reading it makes one very happy. It makes one happy because it renders one in imagination a sharer of that splendid sacrifice, that solemn pride, that divine consolation. It makes one happy because it uplifts the heart and purges it of private interests, and admits one into the higher, and more spacious, and grander life of the nation. For my purposes I am not writing an anti-climax when I say that it makes one happy because it is the perfect expression of a deep, grave, and noble emotion, which is the supreme triumph of the expressive arts. It is the work of a great artist. Was it Lincoln? Or was it the America of our dreams? It was the voice of the true emancipator of our art, who will always understand that his task is not to set Beauty and Puritanism at logger-heads, but to make Puritanism beautiful.

II

WHAT IS A PURITAN?

The world is full of renunciations and apprenticeships, and this is thine; thou must pass for a fool and a churl for a long season.

SMALL-CAPS-EMERSON.

Built of furtherance and pursuing,
Not of spent deeds, but of doing.
Silent rushes the swift Lord
Through ruined systems still restored.

EMERSON.

WHAT IS A PURITAN?

The first step towards making Puritanism beautiful is to free the word from exclusive association with the manners and morals of any particular period. Puritanism is not a fixed form of life; it is a formative spirit, an urgent exploring and creative spirit. And so the shape of the Puritan cannot be cast in bronze for all time. He is an iconoclast, an image-breaker; and when he is convicted of self-idolatry, he is the first, beautiful and strong in wrath, to raise the hammer and shatter his own image. Strike at the shadowy incarnations of him around the witch fires of history: he offers you a sharper sword. A hard man in this or any age to keep pace with or to understand.

Both the contemporary and the historical Puritan are still involved in clouds of libel, of which the origins lie in the copious fountains of indiscriminating abuse poured out upon the Puritans of the seventeenth century by great Royalist writers like Butler, Dryden, and Ben Jonson. The Puritan of that day was ordinarily represented by his adversaries as a dishonest casuist and a hypocrite. To illustrate this point, I will produce a brilliantly malevolent portrait from Jonson's comedy, *Bartholomew Fair*.

This play was performed in London six years before the Pilgrims landed at Plymouth; and it helps one to understand why the migratory movement of the day was rather to than from America. Jonson presents a group of Puritans visiting the Fair. Their names are Zeal-of-the-land Busy, Dame Purecraft, and Win-the-fight Little-wit and his wife. Roast pig is a main feature of the Bartholomew festivities; and the wife of Win-the-fight Little-wit feels a strong inclination to partake of it. Her mother, Dame Purecraft, has some scruples about eating in the tents of wickedness, and carries the question to Zeal-of-the-land Busy, asking him to resolve their doubts. At first he replies adversely, in the canting, sing-song nasal fashion then attributed to the Puritans by their enemies:—

'Verily for the disease of longing, it is a disease, a carnal disease, or appetite . . . and as it is carnal and incident, it is natural, very natural; now pig, it is a meat, and a meat that is nourishing and may be longed for, and so consequently eaten; it may be eaten; very exceedingly well eaten; but in the Fair, and as a Barthol-

omew pig, it cannot be eaten; for the very calling it a Bartholomew pig, and to eat it so, is a
spice of idolatry, and you make the Fair no better than one of the high-places. This, I take
it, is the state of the question: a high-place.'

Master Little-wit remonstrates, saying, 'But
in state of necessity, place should give place,
Master Busy.' And Dame Purecraft cries:
'Good brother Zeal-of-the-land Busy, think to
make it as lawful as you can.'

Thereupon, Zeal-of-the-land Busy reconsid-
ers, as follows:—

'Surely, it may be otherwise, but it is subject
to construction, subject, and hath a face of
offence with the weak, a great face, a foul face;
but that face may have a veil put over it, and
be shadowed as it were; it may be eaten, and in
the Fair, I take it, in a booth, the tents of the
Wicked: the place is not much, not very much,
we may be religious in the midst of the profane,
so it be eaten with a reformed mouth, with
sobriety and humbleness; not gorged in with
gluttony or greediness, there's the fear: for,
should she go there, as taking pride in the place,
or delight in the unclean dressing, to feed the
vanity of the eye, or lust of the palate, it were
not well, it were not fit, it were abominable and
not good.'

Finally, Zeal-of-the-land Busy not only con-
sents, but joins the rest, saying, 'In the way of
comfort to the weak, I will go and eat. I will
eat exceedingly and prophesy; there may be a
good use made of it too, now I think on it: by
the public eating of swine's flesh, to profess our
hate and loathing of Judaism, whereof the
brethren stand taxed. I will therefore eat, yea,
I will eat exceedingly.'

The entire passage might be regarded as a
satirical interpretation of Calvin's chapter on
Christian Liberty. In this fashion the anti-
Puritan writers of the seventeenth century habitually depicted the people who set up the Commonwealth in England and colonized Massa-
chusetts. In the eyes of unfriendly English
contemporaries, the men who came over in the
Mayflower and their kind were unctuous
hypocrites.

That charge, though it has been revived for
modern uses, no longer stands against the seventeenth-century Puritans. Under persecution
and in power, on the scaffold, in war, and in
the wilderness, they proved that, whatever their
faults, they were animated by a passionate sincerity. When the Puritan William Prynne
spoke disrespectfully of magistrates and bishops, Archbishop Laud, or his agents, cut off his

ears and threw him back into prison. As soon as he could get hold of ink and paper, Prynne sent out from prison fresh attacks on the bishops. They took him out and cut off his ears again, and branded him 'S.L.,' which they intended to signify 'Seditious Libeller'; but he, with the iron still hot in his face and with indignation inspiring, perhaps, the most dazzling pun ever recorded, interpreted the letters to mean, *Stigmata Laudis*. When the Puritans came into power, Prynne issued from his dungeon and helped cut off, not the ears, but the head of Archbishop Laud. After that, less was said about his insincerity. Prynne and his friends had their faults; but lack of conviction and the courage of their conviction were not among them.

When, a hundred years ago, Macaulay wrote his famous passage on the Puritans in the essay on Milton, he tried to do them justice; and he did brush aside the traditional charge of hypocrisy with the contempt which it deserves. But in place of the picture of the oily hypocrite, he set up another picture equally questionable. He painted the Puritan as a kind of religious superman of incredible fortitude and determination, who 'went through the world, like Sir Artegal's iron man Talus with his flail, crushing and trampling down oppressors, mingling with human beings, but having neither part nor lot in human infirmities, insensible to fatigue, to pleasure, and to pain, not to be pierced by any weapon, not to be withstood by any barrier.'

Now this portrait of Macaulay's is executed with far more respect for the Puritan character than Jonson exhibited in his portrait of Zeal-of-the-land Busy. But it is just as clearly a caricature. It violently exaggerates certain harsh traits of individual Puritans under perse-cution and at war; it suppresses all the mild and attractive traits; and Carlyle, with his hero-worship and his eye on Cromwell, continues the exaggeration in the same direction. It gives an historically false impression, because it con-veys the idea that the Puritans were exception-ally harsh and intolerant *as compared with other men in their own times.*

For example, the supposedly harsh Puritan Cromwell stood for a wide latitude of religious opinion and toleration of sects at a time when the Catholic Inquisition had established a rigid censorship and was persecuting Huguenots and Mohammedans and Jews, and torturing and burning heretics wherever its power extended. It is customary now to point to the Salem witch-craft and the hanging of three Quakers in Boston—who incidentally seem to have insisted on being hanged—as signal illustrations of the intolerance of Puritanism and its peculiar fanaticism. But, as a matter of fact, these things were merely instances of a comparatively *mild* infection of the Puritans by a madness that swept over the world. In Salem there were twenty victims, and the madness lasted one year. In Europe there were hundreds of thousands of victims; and there were witches burned in Catholic Spain, years after the practice of executing witches had been condemned among the Puritans. Comparatively speaking, the Puritans were quick to discard and condemn the common harshness and intolerance of their times.

The Puritan leaders in the seventeenth century were, like all leaders, exceptional men; but if looked at closely, they exhibit the full complement of human qualities, and rather more than less than average respect for the rights and the personality of the individual, since their doctrines, political and religious, immensely emphasized the importance and sacredness of the individual life. They had iron enough in their blood to put duty before pleasure; but that does not imply that they banished pleasure. They put goodness above beauty; but that does not mean that they despised beauty.   It does not set them apart as a peculiar and abnormal people.   In every age of the world, in every progressing society, there is, there has to be, a group, and a fairly large group, of leaders and toilers to whom their own personal pleasure is a secondary consideration—a consideration secondary to the social welfare and the social advance.   On the long slow progress of the race out of Egypt into the Promised Land, they prepare the line of march, they look after the arms and munitions, they bring up the supplies, they scout out the land, they rise up early in the morning, they watch at night, they bear the burdens of leadership, while the children, the careless young people, and the old people who have never grown up, are playing or fiddling or junketing on the fringes of the march.   They are never popular among these who place pleasure first; for they are always rounding up stragglers, recalling loiterers, and preaching up the necessity of toil and courage and endurance.   They are not popular; but they are not inhuman.   The violet smells to them as it does to other men; and rest and recreation are as sweet.   I must illustrate a little the more intimately human aspect of our seventeenth-century group.

It is a part of the plot of our droll and **dry**

young people to throw the opprobrium of the present drought upon the Puritans. These iron men, one might infer from reading the discourses, for example, of Mr. Mencken, banished wine as a liquor inconsistent with Calvinistic theology, though, to be sure, Calvin himself placed it among 'matters indifferent.' The Puritans, as a matter of fact, used both wine and tobacco—both men and women. If Puritanism means reaction in favor of obsolete standards, our contemporary Puritans will repeal the obnoxious amendment; and all who are thirsty should circulate the Puritan literature of the seventeenth century. Read your *Pilgrim's Progress,* and you will find that Christian's wife, on the way to salvation, sent her child back after her bottle of liquor. Read Winthrop's letters, and you will find that Winthrop's wife writes to him to thank him for the tobacco that he has sent to her mother. Read Mather's diary, and you will find that he suggests pious thoughts to be meditated upon by the members of his household while they are engaged in home brewing. Read the records of the first Boston church, and you will find that one of the first teachers was a wine seller. Read the essays of John Robinson, first pastor of the Pilgrims, and you will find that he ridicules

Lycurgus, the Spartan lawgiver, for ordering the vines cut down, merely 'because men were sometimes drunken with the grapes.' Speaking of celibacy, Robinson says, 'Abstinence from marriage is no more a virtue than abstinence from wine or other pleasing natural thing. Both marriage and wine are of God and good in themselves.'

Since I do not wish to incite a religious and Puritanical resistance to the Volstead Act, I must add that Robinson, in that tone of sweet reasonableness which characterizes all his essays, remarks further: 'Yet may the abuse of a thing be so common and notorious and the use so small and needless as better want the small use than be in continual danger of the great abuse.' And this, I suppose, is exactly the ground taken by the sensible modern prohibitionist. It is not a matter of theological sin with him at all. It never was that. When it is not a question of health, it is now a matter of economics and æsthetics, and of the greatest happiness and freedom to the greatest number.

These iron men are accused of being hostile to beauty, the charge being based upon the crash of a certain number of stained-glass windows and altar ornaments, which offended them, however, not as art, but as religious symbolism.

Why fix upon the riot of soldiers in war-time and neglect to inquire: Who, after the death of Shakespeare, in all the seventeenth century, most eloquently praised music and the drama? Who most lavishly described and most exquisitely appreciated nature? Who had the richest literary culture and the most extensive acquaintance with poetry? Who published the most magnificent poems? The answer to all these questions is, of course, that conspicuous Puritan, the Latin secretary to Oliver Cromwell, John Milton.

In a letter to an Italian friend, Milton writes: 'God has instilled into me, if into anyone, a vehement love of the beautiful. Not with so much labor is Ceres said to have sought her daughter Proserpine, as it is my habit day and night to seek for this idea of the beautiful . . . through all the forms and faces of things.' With some now nearly obsolete notions of precedence, Milton did place God before the arts. But was he hostile to the arts? The two most important sorts of people in the state, he declares, are, first, those who make the social existence of the citizens 'just and holy,' and, second, those who make it 'splendid and beautiful.' He insists that the very stability of the state depends upon the splendor and excellence of its public institutions and the splendid and excellent expression of its social life—depends, in short, as, I have insisted, upon the coöperation of the Puritans and the artists, upon the integrity of the national genius.

These iron men are said to have been devoid of tenderness and sympathy in personal relations. But this does not agree with the testimony of Bradford, who records it in his history that, in the first winter at Plymouth, when half the colony had died and most of the rest were sick, Myles Standish and Brewster, and the four or five others who were well, watched over and waited on the rest with the loving tenderness and the unflinching fidelity of a mother.

These people had fortitude; but was it due to callousness? Were they really, as Macaulay intimates, insensible to their own sufferings and the sufferings of others? Hear the cry of John Bunyan when prison separates him from his family: 'The parting with my wife and poor children hath often been to me in this place as the pulling the flesh from my bone; and that not only because I am somewhat too fond of these great mercies, but also because I should have often brought to my mind the many hardships, miseries, and wants that my poor family was like to meet with, should I be taken from them, *especially my poor blind child,* who lay nearer my heart than all I had besides.   O the thought of the hardship I thought my blind one might go under, would break my heart to pieces.'

Finally, these iron men are grievously charged with a lack of romantic feeling and the daring necessary to act upon it.   Much depends upon what you mean by romance.   If you mean by romance, a life of excitement and perilous adventure, there are duller records than that of the English Puritans.   Not without some risk to themselves, not without at least an occasional thrill, did these pious villagers decapitate the King of England, overturn the throne of the Archbishop of Canterbury, pull up stakes and settle in Holland, sail the uncharted Atlantic in a cockleshell, and set up a kingdom for Christ in the howling wilderness.   I don't think that dwellers in Gopher Prairie or Greenwich Village have a right to call that life precisely humdrum.

Add to this the fact that the more fervent Puritans were daily engaged in a terrifically exciting adventure with Jehovah. Some women of to-day would think it tolerably interesting, I should suppose, to be married to a man like Cotton Mather, who rose every day after breakfast, went into his study, put, as he said, his sinful mouth in the dust of his study floor, and, while the tears streamed from his eyes, conversed directly with angels, with 'joy unspeakable and full of glory.' If a Puritan wife was pious, she was engaged in a true 'eternal triangle'; when Winthrop left home, his wife was committed by him to the arms of her heavenly lover. If she were not pious, she stole the records of his conversation with angels, and went, like Mather's wife, into magnificent fits of jealousy against the Lord of Hosts. The resulting atmosphere may not have been ideal; but it is not to be described as 'sullen gloom'; it was not humdrum like a Dreiser novel; it was tense with the excitement of living on the perilous edge of Paradise.

Did these Puritan husbands lack charm, or devotion to their women? I find that theory hard to reconcile with the fact that so many of them had three wives. Most of us modern men feel that we have charm enough, if we can obtain and retain one, now that higher education of women has made them so exacting in their standards and so expensive to maintain. Now, Cotton Mather had three wives; and when he was forty or so, in the short interim between number two and number three, he received a proposal of marriage from a girl of twenty, who was, he thought, the wittiest and

the prettiest girl in the colony. I conclude
inevitably that there was something very attractive in Cotton Mather. Call it charm; call it
what you will; he possessed that which the
Ladies' Home Journal would describe as 'What
women admire in men.'

As a further illustration of the 'sullen gloom
of their domestic habits,' take the case of John
Winthrop, the pious Puritan governor of Mas-
sachusetts. After a truly religious courtship,
he married his wife, about 1618, against the
wishes of her friends. We have some letters of
the early years of their life together, in which
he addresses her as 'My dear wife,' 'My sweet
wife,' and 'My dear wife, my chief joy in this
world.' Well, that is nothing; at first, we all
do that.

But ten years later Winthrop prepared to visit
New England, without his family, to found a
colony. While waiting for his ship to sail, he
writes still to his wife by every possible mes-
senger, merely to tell her that she is his chief
joy in all the world; and before he leaves England he arranges with her that, as long as he is
away, every week on Tuesday and Friday at
five o'clock he and she shall think of each other
wherever they are, and commune in spirit.
When one has been married ten or twelve long

years, that is more extraordinary. It shows, I think, romantic feeling equal to that in *Miss Lulu Bett,* or *Poor White,* or *Moon-Calf.*

Finally, I will present an extract from a letter of this same John Winthrop to this same wife, written in 1637, when they had been married twenty years. It is an informal note, written hurriedly, in the rush of business:—

Sweeetheart,—

I was unwillingly hindered from coming to thee, nor am I like to see thee before the last day of this weeke: therefore I shall want a band or two: and cuffs. I pray thee also send me six or seven leaves of tobacco dried and powdered. Have care of thyself this cold weather, and speak to the folks to keep the goats well out of the garden. . . . If any letters be come for me, send them by this bearer. I will trouble thee no further. The Lord bless and keep thee, my sweet wife, and all our family; and send us a comfortable meeting. So I kiss thee and love thee ever and rest

Thy faithful husband,
John Winthrop.

If, three hundred years after my death, it is proved by documentary evidence that twenty years after my marriage I still, in a familiar note, mixed up love and kisses with my collars and tobacco—if this is proved, I say, I shall feel very much surprised if the historian of that day speaks of the 'sullen gloom of my domestic habits.'

But now, three hundred years after Winthrop's time, what is actually being said about the Puritans? In spite of abundant evidences such as I have exhibited, our recent Pilgrim celebration was a rather melancholy affair. From the numerous commemoratory articles which I have read, I gather that there are only three distinct opinions about the Puritan now current—every one of them erroneous.

The first, held by a small apologetic group of historians and Mayflower descendants, is, that the Puritan was a misguided man of good intentions. Since he was a forefather and has long been dead, he should be spoken of respectfully; and it is proper from time to time to drop upon his grave a few dried immortelles. The second opinion is, that the Puritan was an unqualified pest, but that he is dead and well dead, and will trouble us no more forever. The third, and by far the most prevalent, is, that the Puritan was once a pest, but has now become a menace; that he is more alive than ever, more baleful, more dangerous.

This opinion is propagated in part by old New Englanders like Mr. Brooks Adams, who have turned upon their ancestors with a vengeful fury, crying, 'Tantum religio potuit suadere malorum.' And I noticed only the other day that Mr. Robert Herrick was speaking remorsefully of Puritanism as an 'ancestral blight' in his veins. But the opinion is still more actively propagated by a literary group which comes out flatfootedly against the living Puritan as the enemy of freedom, of science, of beauty, of romance; as a being with unbreakable belief in his own bleak and narrow views; a Philistine, a hypocrite, a tyrant, of savage cruelty of attack, with a lust for barbarous persecution, and of intolerable dirty-mindedness.

Despite the 'plank' of universal sympathy in the rather hastily constructed literary platform of these young people, it is manifest that they are out to destroy the credit of the Puritan in America. We are not exceptionally rich in spiritual traditions. It would be a pity, by a persistent campaign of abuse, to ruin the credit of any good ones. One of the primary functions, indeed, of scholarship and letters is to connect us with the great traditions and to inspire us with the confidence and power which result from such a connection. Puritanism, rightly understood, is one of the vital, progressive, and enriching human traditions. It is a tradition peculiarly necessary to the health and the stability and the safe forward movement of a democratic society. When I consider from what antiquity it has come down to us and what vicissitudes it has survived, I do not fear its extermination; but I resent the misapprehension of its character and the aspersion of its name. Perhaps our insight into its true nature may be strengthened and our respect renewed, if we revisit its source and review its operations at some periods a little remote from the dust and diatribes of contemporary journalism.

A good many ages before Rome was founded, or Athens, or ancient Troy, or Babylon, or Nineveh, there was an umbrageous banyan tree in India, in whose wide-spreading top and populous branches red and blue baboons, chimpanzees, gorillas, orang-outangs, and a missing group of anthropoid apes had chattered and fought and flirted and feasted and intoxicated themselves on cocoanut wine for a thousand years. At some date which I can't fix with accuracy, the clatter and mess and wrangling of arboreal simian society began to pall on the heart of one of the anthropoid apes. He was not happy. He was afflicted with ennui. He felt stirring somewhere in the region of his diaphragm a yearning and capacity for a new life. His ideas were vague; but he resolved to make a break for freedom and try an experiment. He crawled nervously out to the end of his branch, followed by a few of his friends, hesitated a moment; then exclaimed abruptly: 'Here's where I get off,' dropped to the ground, lighted on his feet, and amid a pelting of decayed fruit and cocoanut shells and derisive shouts of 'precisian' and 'hypocrite,' walked off on his hind-legs into another quarter of the jungle and founded the human race. That was the first Puritan.

In the beginning, he had only a narrow vision; for his eyes were set near together, as you will see if you examine his skull in the museum. He had a vision of a single principle, namely, that he was to go upright, instead of on all fours. But he gradually made that principle pervade all his life; for he resolutely refrained from doing anything that he could not do while going upright. As habit ultimately made the new posture easy and natural, he found that there were compensations in it; for he learned to do all sorts of things in the erect attitude that he

could not do, even with the aid of his tail, while
he went on all-fours.   So he began to rejoice in
what he called 'the new freedom.'   But to the
eyes of the denizens of the banyan tree, he looked
very ridiculous.   They called him stiff-necked,
strait-laced, unbending, and inflexible.   They
swarmed into his little colony of come-outers,
on all fours, and began to play their monkey-
tricks.   He met them gravely and said: 'Walk
upright, as the rest of us do, and you may stay
and share alike with us.   Otherwise, out you
go.'   And out some of them went, back to the
banyan tree; and there, with the chimpanzees
and the red and blue baboons, they still chatter
over their cocoanut wine, and emit from time
to time a scream of simian rage, and declare
their straight-backed relative a tyrant, a despot,
and a persecutor of his good old four-footed
cousins.

You may say that this is only a foolish fable.
But it contains all the essential features of the
eternal Puritan: namely, dissatisfaction with
the past, courage to break sharply from it, a
vision of a better life, readiness to accept a
discipline in order to attain that better life, and
a serious desire to make that better life prevail
—a desire reflecting at once his sturdy individu-
alism and his clear sense for the need of social

solidarity.   In these respects all true Puritans, in all ages and places of the world, are alike. Everyone is dissatisfied with the past; everyone has the courage necessary to revolt; everyone has a vision; everyone has a discipline; and everyone desires his vision of the better life to prevail.

How do they differ among themselves?   They differ in respect to the breadth and the details of their vision.   Their vision is determined by the width of their eyes and by the lights of their age.   According to the laws of human development, some of the lights go out from time to time, or grow dim, and new lights appear, and the vision changes from age to age.

What does not change in the true Puritan is the passion for improvement.   What does not change is the immortal urgent spirit that breaks from the old forms, follows the new vision, seriously seeks the discipline of the higher life. When you find a man who is quite satisfied with the past and with the routine and old clothes of his ancestors, who has not courage for revolt and adventure, who cannot accept the discipline and hardship of a new life, and who does not really care whether the new life prevails, you may be sure that he is not a Puritan.

But who are the Puritans?   Aristotle recognized that there is an element of the Puritan in every man, when he declared that all things, by an intuition of their own nature, seek their perfection. He classified the desire for perfection as a fundamental human desire. Still, we have to admit that in many men it must be classified as a victoriously suppressed desire. We can recognize men as Puritans only when they have released and expressed their desire for perfection.

Leopardi declared that Jesus was the first to condemn the world as evil, and to summon his followers to come out from it, in order to found a community of the pure in heart. But this is an historical error. Unquestionably Jesus was a Puritan in relation to a corrupt Jewish tradition and in relation to a corrupt and seriously adulterated pagan tradition. But every great religious and moral leader, Christian or pagan, has likewise been a Puritan: Socrates, Plato, Zeno, Confucius, Buddha. Every one of them denounced the world, asked his followers to renounce many of their instinctive ways, and to accept a rule and discipline of the better life—a rule involving a purification by the suppression of certain impulses and the liberation of others.

There is much talk of the austerities of the

Puritan households of our forefathers, austerities which were largely matters of necessity. But two thousand years before these forefathers, there were Greek Stoics, and Roman Stoics, and Persian and Hindu ascetics, who were far more austere, and who practised the ascetic life from choice as the better life. There is talk as if Protestant Calvinism had suddenly in modern times introduced the novel idea of putting religious duty before gratification of the senses. But a thousand years before Knox and Calvin, there were Roman Catholic monasteries and hermitages, where men and women, with a vision of a better life, mortified the flesh far more bitterly than the Calvinists ever dreamed of doing. If contempt of earthly beauty and earthly pleasure were the work of Puritanism, then the hermit saints of Catholicism who lived before Calvin should be recognized as the model Puritans. But the hermit saint lacks that passion for making his vision prevail, lacks that practical sense of the need for social solidarity, which are eminent characteristics of the true Puritan, both within and without the Roman Church.

In the early Middle Ages the Roman Church, which also had a strong sense of the need for social solidarity, strove resolutely to keep the

Puritans, whom it was constantly developing, within its fold and to destroy those who escaped. If I follow the course of those who successfully left the fold, it is not because many did not remain within; it is because the course of those who came out led them more directly to America.

In the fourteenth century, John Wycliffe, the first famous English Puritan, felt that the Roman Church had become hopelessly involved with the 'world' on the one hand, and with unnatural, and therefore unchristian, austerities on the other, and that, in both ways, it had lost the purity of the early Christian vision of the better life. To obtain freedom for the better life, he became convinced that one must come out from the Roman Church, and must substitute for the authority of the pope the authority of the Bible as interpreted by the best scholarship of the age. He revolted, as he thought, in behalf of a life, not merely more religious, but also more actively and practically moral, and intellectually more honest. For him, accepting certain traditional doctrines meant acquiescence in ignorance and superstition. His followers, with the courage characteristic of their tradition, burned at the stake rather than profess faith in a 'feigned miracle.'

True forerunners, they were, of the man of science who 'follows truth wherever it leads.'

A hundred and fifty years later the English Church as a whole revolted from the Roman, on essentially the grounds taken by Wycliffe; and under Mary its scholars and ministers by scores burned at the stake for their vision of the better life, which included above all what they deemed intellectual integrity. At that time, the whole English Church was in an essentially Puritan mood, dissatisfied with the old, eager to make the new vision prevail, fearless with the courage of the new learning, elate with the sense of national purification and intellectual progress.

But the word Puritan actually came into use first after the Reformation. It was applied in the later sixteenth century to a group within the English Church which thought that the national church had still insufficiently purged itself of Roman belief and ritual. Among things which they regarded as merely traditional and unscriptural, and therefore unwarrantable, was the government of the church by bishops, archdeacons, deacons, and the rest—the Anglican hierarchy. And when these officers began to suppress their protests, these Puritans began to feel that the English Church was too much involved with the world to permit them freedom for the prac-

tice of the better life. Accordingly, in the
seventeenth century, they revolted as noncon-
formists or as separatists; and drew off into
religious communities by themselves, with
church governments of representative or democratic character, the principles of which were
soon to be transferred to political communities.

If I recall here what is very familiar, it is to
emphasize the swift, unresting onward movement of the Puritan vision of the good life.
The revolt against the bishops became a revolution which shook the pillars of the Middle Ages
and prepared the way for modern times. The
vision, as it moves, broadens and becomes more
inclusive. For the seventeenth-century Puritan,
the good life is not merely religious, moral, and
intellectual; it is also, in all affairs of the soul,
a self-governing life. It is a free life, subject
only to divine commands which each individual
has the right to interpret for himself. The
Puritan minister had, to be sure, a great influence; but the influence was primarily due to his
superior learning. And the entire discipline of
the Puritans tended steadily towards raising the
congregation to the level of the minister. Their
daily use of the Bible, their prompt institution
of schools and universities, and the elaborate
logical discourses delivered from the pulpits

constituted a universal education for independent and critical free-thought.

Puritanism made every man a reasoner. And much earlier than is generally recognized, the Puritan mind began to appeal from the letter to the spirit of Scripture, from Scripture to scholarship, and from scholarship to the verdict of the philosophic reason. Says the first pastor of the Pilgrims: 'He that hath a right philosophical spirit and is but morally honest would rather suffer many deaths than call a pin a point or speak the least thing against his understanding or persuasion.' In John Robinson we meet a man with a deep devotion to the truth, and also with the humility to recognize clearly that he possesses but a small portion of truth. He conceives, indeed, of a truth behind the Bible itself, a truth which may be reached by other means than the Scripture, and which was not beyond the ken of the wise pagans. 'All truth,' he declares, 'is of God. . . . Whereupon it followeth that nothing true in right reason and sound philosophy can be false in divinity. . . . I add, though the truth be uttered by the devil himself, yet it is originally of God.'

The delightful aspects of this 'Biblical Puritan,' besides the sweetness of his charity and his tolerance, are his lively perception that truth is something growing, steadily revealing itself, breaking upon us like a dawn; and, not less significant, his recognition that true religion must be in harmony with reason and experience. 'Our Lord Christ,' he remarks—quietly yet memorably—'calls himself truth, *not custom.'*

Cotton Mather, partly because of his connection with the witchcraft trials, has been so long a synonym for the unlovely features of the culture of his time and place, that even his biographer and the recent editors of his journal have quite failed to bring out the long stride that he made towards complete freedom of the mind. If the truth be told, Mather, like every Puritan of powerful original force, was something of a 'heretic.' For many years he followed a plainly mystical 'inner light.' His huge diary opens in 1681 with a statement that he has come to a direct agreement with the Lord Jesus Christ, and that no man or book, but the spirit of God, has shown him the way. He goes directly to the several persons of the Trinity, and transacts his business with them or with their ministering angels. There is an 'enthusiastic' element here; but one should observe that it is an emancipative element.

Experience, however, taught Mather a certain distrust of the mystical inner light. Experience with witches taught him a certain wariness of angels. In 1711, after thirty years of active service in the church, Mather writes in his diary this distinctly advanced criterion for inspiration:—

'There is a thought which I have often had in my mind; but I would now lay upon my mind a charge to have it oftener there: that the light of reason is the law of God; the voice of reason is the voice of God; we never have to do with reason, but at the same time we have to do with God; our submission to the rules of reason is an obedience to God. Let me as often as I have evident reason set before me, think upon it; the great God now speaks to me.'

Our judgment of Mather's vision must depend upon what reason told Mather to do. Well, every day of his life reason told Mather to undertake some good for his fellow men. At the beginning of each entry in his diary for a long period of years stand the letters 'G. D.,' which mean Good Designed for that day. 'And besides all this,' he declares, 'I have scarce at any time, for these five-and-forty years and more, so come as to stay in any company without considering whether no good might be done before I left it.' One sees in Mather a striking illustration of the Puritan passion for making one's vision of the good life prevail. 'It has been a maxim with me,' he says, 'that a power to do good not only gives a right unto it, but also makes the doing of it a duty. I have been made very sensible that by pursuing of this maxim, I have entirely ruined myself as to this world and rendered it really too hot a place for me to continue in.'

Mather has here in mind the crucial and heroic test of his Puritan spirit. Towards the end of his life, in 1721, an epidemic of small-pox swept over Boston. It was generally interpreted by the pious as a visitation of God. Mather, a student of science as well as of the Bible had read in the *Transactions of the Royal Society* reports of successful inoculation against smallpox practised in Africa and among the Turks. He called the physicians of Boston together, explained the method, and recommended their experimenting with it. He also published pamphlets in favor of inoculation. He was violently attacked as opposing the decrees of God. In the face of a storm of opposition he inoculated his own child, who nearly died of the treatment. None the less, he persisted, and invited others to come into his house and receive the treatment, among them a fellow minister. Into the room where the patient lay, was thrown a bomb intended for Mather, which failed, however, to explode. To it was attached this note: 'Cotton Mather, you dog, damn you; I'll inoculate you with this, with a pox to you!'

Mather stood firm, would not be dissuaded, even courted martyrdom for the new medical truth. 'I had rather die,' he said, 'by such hands as now threaten my life than by a fever; and much rather die for my conformity to the blessed Jesus in essays to save life than for some truths, tho' precious ones, to which many martyrs testified formerly in the flames of Smithfield.'

Here, then, please observe, is the free Puritan mind in revolt, courageously insisting on making his new vision of the good life prevail, resolutely undertaking the discipline and dangers of experiment, and, above all, seeking what he calls the will of the 'blessed Jesus,' not in the Bible, but in a medical report of the Royal Society; thus fulfilling the spirit of Robinson's declaration that 'Our Lord Christ calls himself truth, *not custom';* and illustrating Robinson's other declaration that true religion cannot conflict with right reason and sound experience. In Mather, the vision of the good life came to mean a rational and practical beneficence in

the face of calumny and violence. For his conduct on this occasion, he deserves to have his
sins forgiven, and to be ranked and remembered
as a hero of the modern spirit.

He hoped that his spirit would descend to his
son; but the full stream of his bold and original
moral energy turned elsewhere. There was a
Boston boy of Puritan ancestry, who had sat
under Cotton Mather's father, who had heard
Cotton Mather preach in the height of his
power, and who said years afterward that reading Cotton Mather's book, *Essays to do Good,*
'gave me such a turn of thinking, as to have an
influence on my conduct through life; for I have
always set a greater value on the character of a
doer of good, than on any other kind of reputation; and if I have been . . . a useful citizen, the public owes the advantage of it to that
book.' This boy had a strong common sense.
To him, as to Mather, right reason seemed the
rule of God and the voice of God.

He grew up in Boston under Mather's influence, and became a free-thinking man of the
world, entirely out of sympathy with strait-
laced and stiff-necked upholders of barren rites
and ceremonies. I am speaking of the greatest
liberalizing force in eighteenth-century Amer-

ica, Benjamin Franklin.* Was he a Puritan? Perhaps no one thinks of him as such. Yet we see that he was born and bred in the bosom of Boston Puritanism; that he acknowledges its greatest exponent as the prime inspiration of his life. Furthermore, he exhibits all the essential characteristics of the Puritan: dissatisfaction, revolt, a new vision, discipline, and a passion for making the new vision prevail. He represents, in truth, the reaction of a radical, a living Puritanism, to an age of intellectual enlightenment.

Franklin began his independent effort in a revolt against ecclesiastical authority, as narrow and unrealistic. Recall the passage in his Autobiography where he relates his disgust at a sermon preached on the great text in Philippians: "Whatsoever things are true, honest, just, pure, lovely, or of good report, if there be any virtue, or any praise, think on these things." Franklin says that, in expounding this text, the minister confined himself to five points: keeping the Sabbath, reading the Scriptures, attending public worship, partaking of the sacraments, and respecting the ministers. Franklin recognized at once that there was no moral life in

---

* In presenting this sketch of the Puritan tradition in America, I apologize for the necessity of reproducing some paragraphs from my essay on Emerson in *Americans*.

that minister, was 'disgusted,' and attended his preaching no more. It was the revolt of a living Puritanism from a Puritanism that was dead.

For, note what follows, as the consequence of his break with the church. 'It was about this time that I conceived,' says Franklin, 'the bold and arduous project of arriving at moral perfection. I wished to live without committing any fault at any time, and to conquer all that either natural inclination, custom, or company might lead me into.' Everyone will recall how Franklin drew up his table of the thirteen real moral virtues, and how diligently he exercised himself to attain them. But, for us, the significant feature of his enterprise was the realistic spirit in which it was conceived: the bold attempt to ground the virtues on reason and experience rather than authority; the assertion of his doctrine 'that vicious actions are not hurtful because they are forbidden, but forbidden because they are hurtful, *the nature of man alone considered.*'

Having taken this ground, it became necessary for him to explore the nature of man and the universe. So Puritanism, which, in Robinson and Mather, was predominantly rational, becomes in Franklin predominantly scientific.

With magnificent fresh moral force, he seeks for the will of God in nature, and applies his discoveries with immense practical benevolence to ameliorating the common lot of mankind, and to diffusing good-will among men and nations. Light breaks into his mind from every quarter of his century. His vision of the good life includes bringing every faculty of mind and body to its highest usefulness. With a Puritan emancipator like Franklin, we are not obliged to depend, for the opening of our minds, upon subsequent liberators devoid of his high reconstructive seriousness.

I must add just one more name, for the nineteenth century, to the history of our American Puritan tradition. The original moral force which was in Mather and Franklin passed in the next age into a man who began to preach in Cotton Mather's church, Ralph Waldo Emerson, descendant of many generations of Puritans. The church itself had now become Unitarian: yet, after two or three years of service, Emerson, like Franklin, revolted from the church; the vital force of Puritanism in him impelled him to break from the church in behalf of his vision of sincerity, truth, and actuality. 'Whoso would be a man,' he declared in his famous essay on Self-Reliance, 'must be a

nonconformist. He who would gather immortal palms must not be hindered by the *name*
of goodness, but must explore if it be goodness.'

No American ever lived whose personal life
was more exemplary; or who expressed such
perfect disdain of out-worn formulas and life-
less routine. There is dynamite in his doctrine
to burst tradition to fragments, when tradition
has become an empty shell. 'Every actual state
is corrupt,' he cries in one of his dangerous
sayings; 'good men will not obey the laws too
well.' To good men whose eyes are wide and
full of light, there is always breaking a new
vision of right reason, which is the will of God,
and above the law. Emerson himself broke
the Fugitive Slave Law, and in the face of
howling Pro-Slavery mobs declared that John
Brown would 'make the gallows glorious like
the cross.'

That is simply the political aspect of his
radical Puritanism. On the æsthetic side,
Emerson disregarded the existing conventions
of poetry to welcome Walt Whitman, who
saluted him as master. Emerson hailed Walt
Whitman because Whitman had sought to make
splendid and beautiful the religion of a Puritan
democracy; and a Puritan democracy is the only
kind that we have reason to suppose will endure.

Let these two examples of Emerson's revolt and vision suffice to illustrate the modern operation of the Puritan spirit, its disdain for formalism and routine.

Now, our contemporary leaders of the attack against the modern Puritan declare that modern Puritanism means campaigns of 'snorting and suppression.' That, we should now be prepared to assert, is precisely and diametrically opposite to what modern Puritanism means. Modern Puritanism means the release, not the suppression, of power, welcome to new life, revolt from decay and death. With extravagant asceticism, with precisianism, modern Puritanism has nothing whatever to do.

What made the teaching of Emerson, for example, take hold of his contemporaries, what should commend it to us to-day, is just its unfailingly positive character; its relish for antagonisms and difficulty; its precept for the use of the spur; its restoration of ambition to its proper place in the formation of the manly character; its power to free the young soul from the fetters of fear and send him on his course like a thunder-bolt; and, above all, its passion for bringing the whole of life for all men to its fullest and fairest fruit; its passion for emancipating, not merely the religious and

moral, but also the intellectual and the political
and social and æsthetic capacities of man, so that
he may achieve the harmonious perfection of
his whole nature, body and soul. To this vision
of the good life, Puritanism has come by inevitable steps in its pilgrimage through the
ages.

What have I been trying to demonstrate by
this long review of the Puritan tradition? This,
above all: that the Puritan is profoundly in
sympathy with the modern spirit, is indeed the
formative force in the modern spirit.

In order to make this point perfectly clear,
I must take the liberty of repeating here what
I have already said elsewhere by way of a
description of the modern spirit:

"A great part of our lives, as we all feel in
our educational period, is occupied with learning how to do and to be what others have been
and have done before us. But presently we discover that the world is changing around us, and
that the secrets of the masters and the experience
of our elders do not wholly suffice to establish
us effectively in our younger world. We discover within us needs, aspirations, powers, of
which the generation that educated us seems
unaware, or towards which it appears to be indifferent, unsympathetic, or even actively hos-

tile. We perceive gradually or with successive shocks of surprise that many things which our fathers declared were true and satisfactory are not at all satisfactory, are by no means true, for us. Then it dawns upon us, perhaps as an exhilarating opportunity, perhaps as a grave and sobering responsibility, that in a little while we ourselves shall be the elders, the responsible generation. Our salvation in the day when we take command will depend, we believe, upon our disentanglement from the lumber of heirlooms and hereditary devices, and upon the free, wise use of our own faculties."

At that moment, if we have inherited, not the Puritan heirlooms, but the living Puritan tradition, we enter into the modern spirit. By this phrase I mean, primarily, "the disposition to accept nothing on authority, but to bring all reports to the test of experience. The modern spirit is, first of all, a free spirit open on all sides to the influx of truth, *even from the past*. But freedom is not its only characteristic. The modern spirit is marked, further, by an active curiosity, which grows by what it feeds upon, and goes ever inquiring for fresher and sounder information, not content till it has the best information to be had anywhere. But since it seeks the best, it is, by necessity, also a critical

spirit, constantly sifting, discriminating, rejecting, and holding fast that which is good, only
till that which is better is within sight. This
endless quest, when it becomes central in a life,
requires labor, requires pain, requires a measure
of courage; and so the modern spirit, with its
other virtues, is an heroic spirit. As a reward
for difficulties gallantly undertaken, the gods
bestow on the modern spirit a kind of eternal
youth, with unfailing powers of recuperation
and growth."

To enter into this spirit is what the Puritan
means by freedom. "He does not, like the false
emancipator, merely cut us loose from the old
moorings and set us adrift at the mercy of wind
and tide. He comes aboard, like a good pilot;
and while we trim our sails, he takes the wheel
and lays our course for a fresh voyage. His
message when he leaves us is not, 'Henceforth
be masterless,' but, 'Bear thou henceforth the
sceptre of thine own control through life and
the passion of life.'" If that message still stirs
us as with the sound of a trumpet, and frees and
prepares us, not for the junketing of a purpose-
less vagabondage, but for the ardor and discipline and renunciation of a pilgrimage, we
are Puritans.

III

A CONVERSATION ON OSTRICHES

*The Reputations of the nineteenth century
will one day be quoted to prove its barbarism.*
EMERSON.

A CONVERSATION ON OSTRICHES

"If the world," said Thorpe in his usual ponderous manner of deepening a light chat by the fireside, "if the world possessed a livelier realistic imagination, it could dispense to advantage with a great part of its idealism." Thorpe is one of the intellectual amphibians developed by the unsettled environment of thought in our times. You know the sort. You can never tell where to have him, for he is always stoutly denying that he is what a moment before you thought he obviously was. "No, no, I'm not a pacifist. Don't class *me* with the Radicals. Why should you think *I'm* opposed to universal military service?" That sort of man.

We had been speaking of the nervous unrest and a kind of mild epidemic hypochondria which were more noticeable through the period of negotiations for peace than they were in the course of the war. "The trouble is," I had suggested, "that we are all suffering from exacerbated imaginations. It is impossible to be cheerful in a constant sense that each one of us is personally responsible for the misgovernment of every Southern European state. We cannot be expected to continue indefinitely responding with a lively pang to every toothache in the Balkans. Of course those who are appointed to the work must clean up the mess. But for the average man in America the motto should now be 'Business as usual.' In his recreative hours he should drop the war books and read Jane Austen's *Emma*. He should abjure the war pictures and visit an Arcadian musical comedy. Seriously, I see no remedy for despair but some form of profoundly attending to one's own business."

"Ostriches!" snorted Thorpe. "You tories are all ostriches. You started the war with your heads in the sand, you got them out towards the end of it, but you won't be happy till you have them snugly in again. Have you seen what Irving Babbitt calls the war?—'the crowning stupidity of the ages.' Babbitt is one of the people who occasionally look at the total human aspect of the thing. What he means is that the entire performance, if held off and scrutinized at arm's length—say, an arm the length of Socrates's—looks like the act of an angry and underbred child. Now the time to punish and admonish a child is when his mischief is fresh in his mind. You are for soothing him with syrups. I don't agree with you. Most of the people I know are already following exactly your prescription. Their nervous unrest is due to the fact that they are trying to have a good time when their consciences tell them that they deserve a thrashing."

"Come, now," I interrupted rather hotly, "don't you admit that the Germans were responsible for the war? When they struck at civilization, what were we to do?"

"Strike back of course," said Thorpe coolly; "but that, I trust, doesn't make it impossible for you to 'regret the entire incident.' The crowning stupidity of the ages might, I should think, without lifting the onus from the chief aggressors, be viewed by all the participants with a considerable measure of regret. I myself find the regretful mood morally so illuminating that I dislike to see it giving way so soon in this country to the post-war festivity. In the case of men who have been in the trenches and hospitals, perhaps a little riot of pleasure and relaxation is as useful as a hypodermic after surgical shock. If I were in Russia, France, or England, probably I should prescribe counter-irritants, lenitives, sedatives. Imaginations there have been cut into deeply enough to hold the impression. But the average American of my acquaintance has been just enough touched by the war to regret that he was not in it. He prepared, indeed, to face the full meaning of battle, but nine out of ten of him faced little more than Jack Fairley did, and stand in as much need of a sweet oblivious antidote."

I could remember nothing of Fairley but his name in a list of men who received their degree *in absentia*—for military service.

"Jack was the best tennis-player in college, the best dresser, the best cheek-to-cheek dancer. Popular son of prosperous father. Not a bad fellow. Clean-cut, well-groomed American type. I met him in the Pullman smoker in war time, full of the big "scrap." He had won a second lieutenancy in the Coast Artillery, but was on leave, and was off with his mandolin, in an admirably fitting uniform, to enliven and decorate some house-party or other. Jack has a flow of spirits, and he told me of the hardships of his camp life by the sea. What I remember is his embarrassment at regulations which made it impossible for him to spend his evenings with certain privates of his company who were also classmates and brethren of his fraternity. For this deprivation, however, he solaced himself at a neighboring sea-side hotel, where every eve·

ning patriotic young women of excellent families and first-rate personal qualifications danced
with the officers, for their country. He told me
that he had two grand ambitions: the first was
to fire his gun in France; the second was to
come home, remove his puttees, and get into a
pair of silk socks again. He has realized the
second; and for the first, though he never got
overseas, he is probably still receiving substantial credit this summer among the fair friends
with whom he is yachting off the Maine coast."

"Well," I inquired, "why shouldn't he?
What do you want to do to Jack—make him
miserable?"

"Not wholly," Thorpe retorted, "but I should
like to send to him—and to his father—for summer reading in the hammock, a copy of Georges
Duhamel's *Civilization, 1914-1917*. It would
stir up an organ in him that the war hasn't
touched yet—his imagination. Have you seen
the book? Goncourt Prize last year. Disquieting, but really worth reading. One of the
notable impressions from the front. It hasn't
the picturesque energy or sullen intensity of
Barbusse. It isn't a merely excruciating picture
of mental and physical horror, like Latzko's
Men in War. And it quite lacks the splendor
of baffled fighting heroism that distinguishes

Masefield's *Gallipoli*. But it takes you overseas and puts you where you can see what went
on here and there. Not the whole story but a
part of it that you are inclined to blink at.
Furthermore, it's literature; it has a personality of its own with a peculiar humor, blend-
ing irony, tenderness, grimness, resignation—
faithfully expressing the mixture of astonish-
ment, curiosity, and dismay with which the
average man in the years of our Lord 1914-
1917 dumbly assisted the lords of the earth in
consigning civilization temporarily—I said
'temporarily'—to the devil."

"I have read the book," I said, "but with
rather less enthusiasm. I must say it affected me
very much as certain chapters in the modern
novels do, chapters that I should like to tear
out, chapters considering with a morbid and un-
holy curiosity and publicity the physiological
processes attendant on an event which in the
older fiction was smilingly reported by physi-
cian or nurse to a man 'pacing restlessly back
and forth in the room below.' I object to these
chapters because they tend to produce extravagant and unnecessary terror before an event
which really must be faced if the agreeable race
to which we belong is to increase and multiply
and spread the blessings of civilization among

the Prussians and other backward peoples. For precisely the same reason I object to Duhamel's book."

"I see," Thorpe broke in, with a rather crudely ironical tone, "for precisely the same reason. Your analogy is flawless. Maternity and war are both necessary, both inevitable, if the race is to continue. You object to deterrents from either. In what German work did you learn of the sacred inevitability of war, the holy duty of handing the torch of battle on from generation to generation? Between deterring people from what is necessary to the perpetuation of life and deterring people from the unnecessary destruction of it, there is, I should think, a not inconsiderable difference."

"You do not, you said, take the radical pacifist position? You aren't ready with Russell to lie down and let the invader swarm over you?"

"No."

"Then admit that the book is dispiriting, demoralizing. It steadily envisages the seamy side of military life without a glimpse of the incontrovertible glamor and glory of battle. That sort of writing is ruinous to morale. It is just what shouldn't be read by a young soldier. It sets the imagination to work. You recall why boys between eighteen and twenty make better soldiers than men of forty: they haven't any imagination. They don't consider what they are getting into, but put their heads down and go in. A man of forty stays awake nights seeing a picture of himself lying in No Man's Land under fire with his leg blown off. Duhamel sets your mind running that way."

"'Civilization,'" Thorpe admitted, "is not the thing to present to a soldier on the way to the front line trenches. It gives too vividly a sense of the sights and smells of the receiving hospital, the operating room, the morgue. But we are not on the way to the trenches now. Jack Fairley is probably reading *The Cosmopolitan* in his hammock at Bar Harbor. Other people, of whom life makes more serious exactions, are soberly reckoning up the profit and loss of the international readjustments we have just been making. There has been even a little fundamental reconsideration of the wisdom of making such adjustments in the manner hitherto fashionable among enlightened people. I should really like to see the matter quite thoroughly overhauled with all available evidence and testimony. The report of a French ambulance surgeon through whose hands the débris of battle drifted to the rear is a legitimate and useful portion of the evidence. I remember hearing a grizzled old Tartar of the Regular Army working up what you call morale in a bunch of young college boys. 'If you're killed,' he told them, 'you're all right. If you're wounded, you're a damn nuisance!' Those college boys all laughed heartily. Now Duhamel makes you understand why, if you're wounded, you're a nuisance."

"And what is the value of that?"

"As a modern realist in an age that prides itself on the remorseless facing of facts, I am in favor of removing the gilded lid of war and looking inside. Somehow I don't fancy this notion of horrors that can only be met by boys who don't know what they are up against. Sending them in savors to me of what I call modern German idealism."

"Please explain," I said, for Thorpe knows no philosophy and uses the terms in odd senses of his own.

"Modern German idealism," said Thorpe, "means retreating from facts into the quieter region of ideas. It means, shut your eyes and everything is lovely. For example, in the days of the Belgian atrocities, the German idealist, we were told, laid this unction to his soul: that the horror of military executions and other harsh punitive measures was mitigated by the fact that those who ordered the sanguinary acts were never the ones who carried them out. It is not clear that this division of responsibility diminishes the horror for the victim. But one readily understands that a cultivated judge who, in the purity of his military idealism, had ordered the shooting of Edith Cavell would sleep the better on the following night if he were not obliged to see the English nurse actually crumple up under the fire of his own rifle. Or, to remove the matter from the hot air of controversy, take the case of Pontius Pilate. As he appears to have been a man of some fineness of sensibility and at the same time tainted with Teutonic idealism, it is more than likely that he refrained from visiting Golgotha to investigate the mere physical consequences of his having washed his hands of responsibility. He withdrew, I suspect, into his own cultivated though somewhat unimaginative mind, and left the eye-witnessing of the thing to a squad of soldiers under orders and to calloused workmen handy with hammer and nails."

"You mean to suggest that if Pilate had possessed a lively imagination, he might not have washed his hands?"

"Just that," said Thorpe. "I attribute the cruelty of his refined nature to his shrinking and cowardly imagination. It is the case of the whole modern world. You shut your eyes and wrap the mantles of your abstract ideas around you and lie down in the midst of horrible realities to pleasant dreams. You can't stand the gaff. Consider how you and other nice men and women shudder away from the deformed and malodorous results of the conflict of your own ideas in these times. I concede that your self-protective idealism has its uses in a crisis. It was the stimulant which made you enter and endure the conflict. It is the opiate which dulls your sense of its pains. It is as busy today as the robins that covered the babes in the woods, weaving a pleasant shroud for dreadful things, hiding them away from the eyes of men for fear of what they might do to the heart if they reached it rawly through the senses."

"Be a little more specific."

"Very well. The only son has given his life for his country. Do not ask for the details. They are distressing. What is left of the only son is brought home for burial. The good clergyman tactfully fixes the attention of father and mother upon the spiritual values preserved by his sacrifice. Over the shattered face the coffin lid is closed. Over the coffin the great flag is draped. Over the grave, smelling too pungently of freshly turned earth, a smother of flowers is strewn. The poet sings of victory. The politicians go forth to address their constituents. And Congress, in the warm afterglow of battle, cheerfully appropriates a million dollars to distribute up and down the land the trophies of the Great War."

"I see nothing objectionable," I said, "in any part of your programme. Everyone seems to be making the best of it. What more can one do? Surely you wouldn't propose harrowing the feelings of the parents who had lost their son by an exhibition or a Zolaesque description of the boy's face."

"No," Thorpe retorted tenaciously, "but I should like to harrow a little the feelings of parents who have not lost their son. I should like to harrow the feelings of Jack Fairley's parents. Already they and ninety per cent. of the American people are beginning to think of those four infernal years as a fairy-tale, with some breathless places in the middle, but coming out all right and happy in the end. In a little while the mere physical reek and wreck will be cleared away, and ten years hence our schoolboys will speak of the year 1914 without a thought of hunger, disease, gas-gangrene, trench fever, lice, or carrion—the spectres which rise in my mind today when I think of those German trophies in the park. The realistic imagination, which for a few bitter months brought these things home to comfortable people in America, will be slumbering again; and the young generation will fancy, as we did once on a time, that war is mainly an affair of flags and heroes and martial music."

"If you are not a pacifist," I said, "you sound remarkably like one. I don't see what you are driving at."

"You're mistaken," Thorpe replied, "I'm not arguing against war. That would be silly. Senator Lodge and General Wood and other idealists insist that we shall have war every little while always; and what such men insist upon is pretty likely to take place. I think, as they do, therefore, that we had better be prepared. Perhaps I believe in an even more comprehensive plan of preparation than theirs. Since they are always talking of the ships and guns, I'm willing to trust them to provide that element. What interests me is that the country should be kept in a state of imaginative preparedness; that is, I want to be sure that it is ready to go in with a clear realistic preliminary vision of costs and consequences, such as never entered the heads, for example, of the military idealists in Germany and Austria. Civilization is now in a horrid predicament from an overdrawn bank account, the result of a shifty, evasive feminine habit of buying and 'charging' all sorts of expensive things without any adequate anticipative facing of the bills. War is a first-class luxury, the cost of which should be contemplated coolly, like the purchase of a yacht or the commission of a crime, to determine whether one can afford it. Too many of my neighbors fancy they are paying for the war when they are only detaching the coupons from their Liberty bonds."

"That is doubtless true," I assented, "but do you know any practical remedy?"

"Whatever," said Thorpe, "stimulates the imagination, that faculty which sees absent things as they really are, will be useful. The German war trophies will help. Duhamel's book will help. I have still another suggestion. In searching the Old Testament along with Mr. Wells and Mr. William Hohenzollern, I have lately been struck with the ingenuity of the ancient Hebrew kings and prophets in driving important matters in on the sluggish imaginations of their countrymen. I refer to the device of cutting a malefactor into twelve pieces and sending a section to each one of the tribes through all the coasts of Israel. Perhaps we ought not to follow this example literally. We might, I think, adapt its leading idea to our modern circumstances. We have at hand a fair number, not of malefactors, but of returned soldiers, already cut up by the enemy in various fashions, some with the loss of a leg, some an arm, some an eye or a nose or a larger segment of the face. What if to each town or village that received a German trophy, Congress should also send, to sit in the park at public expense, one of these more or less fragmentary men? Wouldn't it help unimaginative idealists to make rational estimates for the next war?"

"Thorpe," I said, "I'm glad you're absurd. If you weren't absurd, I shouldn't be at all sure you aren't seditious."

IV

THE SHIFTING
CENTRE OF MORALITY:
A STUDY OF THE VULGAR TONGUE

I say, beware of all enterprises that re-quire new clothes, and not rather a new wearer of clothes. If there is not a new man, how can the new clothes be made to fit? If you have any enterprise before you, try it in your old clothes.

THOREAU.

I do not mean to prescribe rules to strong and valiant natures, who will mind their own affairs whether in heaven or hell, and perchance build more magnificently and spend more lavishly than the richest, without ever impoverishing themselves.

THOREAU.

THE SHIFTING
CENTRE OF MORALITY

If Puritanism is, as I have been contending
that it is, an essentially non-conforming spirit,
then its most formidable adversary should be an
essentially conforming spirit. And contrary to
the general impression of the facts, the spirit in
our present younger generation which is most
deeply at variance with traditional Puritanism
is not its sporadic rebelliousness but its prevailing readiness to conform. Current criticism,
confining itself chiefly to manners and "minor
morals" scents a revolt and a flying-off where a
deeper consideration discovers rather a slavish
conformity.

The social censors have been reporting lately,
in high excitement, that our young people exhibit signs of moral deterioration, that they are
already crowned with vine leaves and dancing
like bacchants down the primrose way. When
one corners a censor and demands point-blank
what is wrong, one is not quite adequately
answered. What one ordinarily receives is an

impressionistic highly-colored account of the débutantes of the present year by a débutante of twenty-five years ago, who ejaculates her indignant "Why-my-dears!" over the vogue of rouge and jazz, the cigarettes and the cocktails, the partial emancipation of the lower (instead of only the upper) limbs, the unchaperoned drives by moonlight, and, in short, the extraordinary accessibility, the general "facility" of the buds. From among these ejaculations there emerges the central assurance of the censor, namely, that she was far, far more difficult to kiss than her neighbor's daughter is. An interesting contention, to which an enquirer of Hamlet's disposition will murmur: "Very like—Very like."

To indict an entire generation on specific charges of this sort is never very convincing. The débutantes who appear at their coming-out parties in bacchantic garb and manners are but an inconsiderable element even in that expensively fashionable set which the Sunday supplement recognizes as Society. And Society itself is but an inconsiderable element in the significant young life of any generation. A small group, flushed and festive, which loves to skirt the perilous verge of decorum, and hang a bit over the edge—such a group is always with us, as any one may easily persuade himself by turning the pages of his Juvenal or his Petrarch or even by running through the files of an illustrated New York weekly from 1860 to 1890. On the basis of rouge and "rag-time" and startling ups and downs of feminine apparel, the ultimate decline of civilization has probably been predicted every thirty years since the time of Queen Semiramis.

The historically-minded critic will be slow to assert that the manners and morals of our younger generation are, on the whole, any worse than those of the older generation, or any better. Yet he may still insist that they are significantly different. For the tendency of young people is to react against both the virtues and the defects of their elders. The father is a hard drinker but the son in disgust resolves not to touch a drop—that sometimes happens. Or the mother reads *The Ladies' Home Journal* and the daughter, *The Liberator*: that also happens. This sort of alternation is not invariable; yet, as we say, an excess in one direction tends to produce an excess in the opposite direction. And between one generation and the next morality does sometimes shift its centre.

Morality has two principal centres.

At one period, we have a morality of which the centre is within the individual. It works from within outward. It holds, like Christianity, that its prime concern is to touch the heart and quicken the conscience and give a right direction to the will. If the heart be right, say the exponents of this morality, right conduct will follow. One does not look to the world for approval; one endeavours to satisfy the inner monitor. One's own standards of right and wrong are more severe than anything that can be imposed from outside. Therefore one takes for a motto: "Trust thyself. To thine own self be true; thou canst not then be false to any man." If you get morality effectively planted at the centre of a man, he does right though no one is looking. He does right though the heavens fall.

The high tendency of this personal morality is to produce a man like Emerson, notable for independence, depth, poise, and serenity. Its low tendency is to produce a sentimentalist like Rousseau, whose "beautiful soul" is dissociated from his mundane and muddy behaviour.

At another period, we have a morality of which the centre is outside the individual. It is felt as a social pressure, working from without inward. It is primarily concerned, like ancient Judaism and like all systems of etiquette, with the regulation of external conduct and manners. When this type of morality predominates, if the actions of a man are right and his manners correct, no one worries much about the condition of his feelings. Act right and right feelings will follow; or if they don't, it doesn't much matter. The watch words are: "Do as the rest do. Conform to established ways. Follow the rules and regulations."

The high tendency of a purely social morality is to cultivate the graces and amenities, and so to produce an urbane and highly polished gentleman like Lord Chesterfield. Its low tendency is to finish the surfaces of character without touching the inward parts, so that the effect upon a sensitive observer, in the case of Talleyrand, was like that of "a silk stocking filled with mud." And an unfriendly critic remarked even of Chesterfield that he taught the "morals of a courtesan and the manners of a dancing master."

Yet let us not forget that this social morality has its merits. It has, above all, a definite method, a perfected technique, for laying hold of the raw uncultivated man and smoothing his surfaces and adjusting his external conduct to an external standard. Everyone has perhaps heard of that lady who always walked into church with such a heavenly smile about her lips that observers thought she must be meditating on some beatific vision, till a friend, more curious than the rest, asked her how she did it. She explained away the mystery by declaring that all she did was to shape her lips, when she entered the church door, as if she were about to utter the word "spruce." The sequel tells how the friend thought to beautify her own expression by the same technique; but she was stopped in the middle of the aisle and was asked in horror, by an acquaintance, what ailed her. She, much chagrined, explained that she was merely trying the formula which had made the beatific lady look so entrancing. "For heaven's sake," cried the neighbor, "what is it?" "Why," she replied, " as I come in the door, I simply shape my lips as if about to utter the word 'hemlock.' "

Both these ladies illustrate very well what I mean by the externality of the method.

At the present time, our ordinary young people are cultivating the external, the socially-centered type of morality. The individual would rather go wrong with the crowd than right by himself. He has a horror of being in any sense alone. He is almost painfully anxious to do as the rest do. Even his "eccentricities"

are stereotyped and fashionable. He "revolts"
by regiments. Three distinct forces tend to
fortify this social morality in a position of predominance over the younger generation: popular philosophy, military discipline, and women.

In the first place, all the popular psycholo-
gists are physiologists, looking upon man as
merely a nervous organism; and all the popular
philosophers are pragmatists, behaviourists,
etc., and occupy themselves with the actions and
reactions, the responses and inhibitions of this
nervous automaton. For them there is no
spiritual centre. For them there is really no inside to personality. Everything is valued in
terms of visible behaviour. Everything gets its
meaning and significance in a network of external relations. Intelligently or otherwise, our
young people seize upon current philosophy to
help them construct an entire universe for themselves which shall have no "insides." In the
violence of their reaction against the idealism
and inwardness of their fathers, they rejoice in
their intention of living on the surface of things.
They will get rid of what their fathers called
sin by getting rid of what their fathers called
the soul.

The heroine of current fiction has no soul—
she has not even a heart; she has only a nervous

system. She has no spiritual crises—she has not even emotional crises; she has only nervous reactions. Our popular novelists—our Floyd Dells and Rose Macauleys, and W. L. Georges and Sinclair Lewises and McFees—never present their heroines in the grip of any such grand passions as shattered the heroines of the Brontë sisters. And yet these modern young women go through far more experiences than Charlotte Brontë ever dreamed it possible for any girl to have. Experiences which would have made the whole of life for Jane Eyre, experiences which would have raised her to rapture or cast her into the nethermost hell,—our modern heroine goes through these at a week-end, and brushes them aside "without batting an eyelid" —as she would say.

The philosophic movement towards an "external" moral centre has doubtless been greatly accelerated by a second force the full consequences of which we are just beginning to feel. It is hardly questionable that army discipline and, perhaps even more, the immense "drives" to which we were subjected in our recent embattled period did much towards establishing in the younger generation its profound deference for this external morality. We hear much about the few dissenters who did not subscribe nor conform, and we hear much about the many honest patriots who did subscribe and conform. But we have had very little study of the effect of military discipline and "drives" upon the vast intermediate mass of unformed plastic young people, practically destitute of individual convictions, who were equipped overnight, by a power not themselves, with uniform convictions and uniform conduct with respect to all manner of subjects which they had never considered.

That abrupt and convulsive shifting of responsibility for belief and conduct from the individual to an organized power outside the individual had its great merits. It frequently clothed the stark naked. But like the asylum that receives the pauper, like the infallible and omniscient church that embraces a thinking soul, it had compensations which were dangers. If you were not in a position of leadership, you had to initiate and decide nothing. You did what the rest did; and you were "all right." Your scruples were cancelled with a rubber stamp. If doubts pursued you, you took refuge in the crowd, which covered you and shaped you. And you quite forget that old individualistic maxim: "We sink as easily as we rise through our sympathies."

How the newly augmented powers of women and their quickened class consciousness will affect the situation in the future remains to be seen; but all experience indicates that these new powers and this quickened class consciousness will tend to fortify the alliance of popular philosophy and military discipline against a personal and internally centered morality. Women in masses are, or always have been, servile under the tyranny of social opinion, and subject to a very gross superstition. Whenever two or three of them are gathered together, the great goddess They is in the midst of them with Her arrogant foot on their necks. There is no woman's club or tea or sewing circle or even domestic fireside where Her voice is not heard and where Her words are not solemnly quoted as oracles, ending with absolute finality all masculine dissent.

It is perhaps within the domestic circle that the tyranny of this deity is most ruthlessly imposed and substituted for the free and natural dictates of the private heart. I will illustrate the procedure. The average man might conceivably dispute, let us assume, with his own wife on fairly equal terms. He has devoted the better part of a lifetime to studying her special tactics and strategems, and knows how to meet them. But the average man is never permitted by a really intelligent wife to carry on any dispute with her. The moment that he begins an argument she softly steps aside—or more accurately, side-steps—and "quotes Scripture," quotes this Hydra-headed monster, Whom it is sacrilege to mention by any other designation than the capitalized third person plural.

At the domestic fireside, argument, as distinguished from conviction, usually begins in a man's soul. In the intimate simplicity of his heart, moved only by considerations of comfort, personal taste, or the family budget, a man will begin thus:

"I believe, Dorothy, we'd better have another electric light put in the dining room, so that we can see a little better what we are taking in."

She will reply: "Oh, no, my dear; we'll do nothing of the sort. They are using candles now."

Or he will begin: "Well, Dotty old dear, I guess the old car will serve us another season, won't it?"

And she: "Why, John, how can you think so? It's quite impossible. They are using closed cars now."

Or the poor man will open a fireside rumination thus: "Do you know, Dorothy, when Kitty's in high school——"

And she will cut in: "But Kitty is not going to the high school. You are absurd. You know perfectly well that They are sending Their girls away to shool now."

Such are the interventions of the great goddess They, trampling rough-shod over the inclinations and powers of the private life. And such is the worship of her, instituted daily on a more and more imposing scale as a large class of timid idolaters becomes a potent organized force in the determination of standards.

Under the combined pressure of philosophy, military discipline, and feminine superstition, the younger generation has been driven to conceive of virtue as merely a facile adjustment to the existing environment. It believes to an excessive degree in certain "standardized" ways of making the adjustment. The resulting phenomena have their comic aspects and their grave aspects, which I shall now explore a little according to a method suggested by this profound aphorism of Stevenson's: "Man lives not by bread alone; but mostly by catchwords." All that is most efficacious in the morality of our time is condensed in its catchwords. I shall hunt for the missing soul of the younger generation by following the bits of slang it has dropped in its flight.

"Abandon hope of social success," I read in an organ of youth a few months ago, "unless you have a car and a 'line.' " For days I enquired in vain of my coevals the meaning of the world 'line.' But the moment I asked a young man of the new times whether he understood it, he laughed, and explained that a 'line' is a complete set of conversational openings and ready-to-wear speeches, practically committed to memory and rehearsed for use on all typical social occasions. If you have a 'line,' you are not at a loss when the door opens, or in the ten minutes' talk with the family or the chaperone, or at any of the difficult transitional moments in your Napoleonic progress from the first dance to the last goodnight.

"It is all right," said my informant, "if you don't go to the same place too often."

I mused on a number of things of which I had read or heard, including the training of a successful bookagent, before I thought of the obvious solution. Then I said: "It sounds like F. Scott Fitzgerald."

"It is like him," he replied. "They all study his stuff—get it by heart. He has the best 'line' going."

I ended my lesson with the understanding that 'line' is short for lifeline, a device by which one avoids the danger of misstepping into the deep water which R. L. Stevenson commended to a former generation of students as "truth of intercourse."

This self-distrust of the new generation, this clinging to the social lifeline, this reliance upon external means of grace, is not confined to undergraduates. It pervades the younger society. It is openly recognized and played upon, for instance, in those popular and entertaining magazines which undertake to teach the newly-rich to spend their money as if they had been rich a long time. "Buy a car," advises a canny caterer to democracy, "which will give you that comfortable sense of superiority." O superlative car! "Here are garments," cries another, "which will put you perfectly at ease in any society." O magical garments! Finally consider a full-page advertisement (in a radical journal which scoffs at decorum) of a book on etiquette, running about like this: "If you spilled a plate of soup in the lap of your hostess, should you apologize profusely, or should you pass over the incident in silence?—Buy this book and find out."

If that old censor of social morals, Thoreau, could visit us and inspect these pages, one can imagine him muttering in his Diogenes' beard:

"Could not a man who really possessed 'a comfortable sense of superiority'—could he not walk? or, if necessary, consider buying a car within his means and adequate to his needs? wear his clothes till they were easy? and, when he spilled the soup, speak what words of consolation God put into his heart?" But Thoreau was of a former generation which sought its comfortable sense of superiority within, rather than in that "ceaseless striving after smartness in clothing," observed by William McFee's London sailor lad as a distinction of the New York man-in-the-street.

Ten thousand finger-posts point the younger generation the way to enter the race for external "distinction," the way to Vanity Fair—ten thousand finger-posts to one honest old-fashioned pilgrim who assures them that it is the privilege of the truly superior man to do what he pleases and what suits his own sense of fitness, simply and nonchalantly. How do heroes converse? "Won't you have a cup of tea?" says King Haakon. "By George, your Majesty," says Mr. Roosevelt, "the very thing I'd like!" You won't find that reply in any book of etiquette; yet it suited the occasion well enough. In general those who always stand on their dignity have nothing else to stand on. It is not the prime minister but the secretarial underlings who step starchily out in frock coats and top hats. Their chief bolts from his office in sack coat and nondescript felt. He has risen above his tailor.

Carlyle had a contemptuous word for all that "superiority" which one can buy at the store: he called it "gigmanity." It is a word that should be taught to our young people as a charm against infatuation with the external show of things. Carlyle found his word in the records of a criminal case. Said a witness: "I have always considered the defendant a respectable man." "What do you mean, sir," queries the judge, "by a respectable man?" "Why, your honor," replied the witness, *"he keeps a gig."* We have substituted for the gig a more elaborate vehicle in which one may ride to respectability—a very smooth-riding vehicle which to be perfectly respectable, should be equipped, according to current standards, with a lap-robe of Chinese civet cat lined with velvet, and an electrically lighted accessories case of gold and pearl.

But consider now a little more closely the young person who expects to be put at ease by a car, a suit of clothes, and a book of etiquette —all of which he recognizes as superior to him-

self. Follow him to college, whither he is sure
to be impelled by his self-distrust and his naive
confidence in a prescribed routine. No organ
within him craves intellectual food; but something without him, a continuous social whisper,
has suggested that there is salvation in a bachelor's degree. College life is a kind of select
soirée, at which it will give him 'a comfortable
sense of superiority' merely to be seen. By him
we explain why academic culture does not
"take." With him in our eye, we expound a
curious phrase in wide use among undergraduates.

Every year I talk with a considerable number
of young persons, about to enter the junior and
senior classes, concerning their program of
studies; and I regularly begin by asking what
they are doing in certain prescribed subjects,
such as foreign languages. Quite regularly
seven out of ten of them answer, with a happy
smile and a reminiscent sigh: "Thank goodness,
I worked *off* my French and German last year."

To which I regularly and hopelessly retort:
"But have you worked *up* your German? Have
you worked *in* your French? We don't require
you to take them for the look of the thing. Can
you use them?"

And they quite regularly respond: "Oh, no!

We don't expect to use them. We merely took them to *work off* group-requirements."

My feigned surprise that they should think us here "for the look of the thing" is an echo, by the way, of Mr. Kipling, who as much as any living writer, gave the tone to undergraduate life twenty years ago. Under the spur of his Indian tales and verse, we talked a good deal in those times about doing the "day's work" without excuses. It was the mode then to admire "men who do things." And so our blood was stirred by Mr. Kipling's hard-mouthed bridge-builder haranguing his shiftless Hindus: "Sons of unthinkable begetting, children of unspeakable shame! Are we here for the look of the thing?"

It is at least twenty years since I read that passage; and yet it vibrates still in the memory with an authority which nothing of Mr. F. Scott Fitzgerald's quite possesses. I will present, on the other hand, a bit of recent dialogue from life, which sounds in my ears like a current tune, expressing the spirit of a new generation which candidly admits that it *is* here "for the look of the thing."

At registration time in the fall a very sweet girl from Georgia with a soft southern voice and soft southern eyes, fringed like jessamine

or honeysuckle, came to me as registration offi-
cer, and asked me to waive a college rule in
her favor.

"I am very sorry," I said, with customary
mild severity, "I can't let you do it. I have no
authority in the matter."

"Well," she replied, "who has? Who can?"
And she looked into my eyes with searching and
almost painful sweetness.

"You might," I said, faltering, "you might
go to the Dean. A Dean is the only one that
breaks rules. You might ask him, but I doubt
if it will do you any good. Our Dean is a very
firm man. He's a New Englander, you know, a
Puritan, with a stiff conscience."

"Tell me something," she said softly, "will
you?"

"Yes," I replied, "if I can." I was ready to
do anything for her, short of breaking the rule.

"Is this Dean of yours a bachelor or a married man?"

"A bachelor," I answered, "a bachelor of
forty."

"Oh, that's all right," she cried gaily, as she
gathered up her papers, "I'll *fix* him."

If, now, you take the spirit of this fair
Georgian and mold it a little under the pressures of the hour, you produce an outstanding

type of the recent feminine "arrivals" in business. She will get on. If she had a shade less
of adaptability and a shade more of "soul," she
would have her difficulties.

I had recently an instructive conversation
with a charming and thoroughly refined young
woman, who, moved by the impulse of her time,
was seeking "economic independence," and had
taken her initial steps in the business world. I
asked her what she had learned from her professional life. "The most important thing that
I have tried to learn," she replied instantly but
without much gusto, "is how to sell myself."

I wish I could say that the vile phrase struck
me as shocking. But how can one be shocked
any longer, whose ears have rung these half-
dozen years with phrases struck at the same
mint, "slogans" of the "nation-wide" "campaigners," "selling charity," "selling art," "selling the war," "selling patriotism," "selling the
flag," "selling the church—yours in business
for the Lord," "selling" things visible and
things invisible, whatever is now for sale in
the heavens above or the waters under the earth
—and everything is for sale. Such is the idiom
of their souls.

At the present moment "production" is looked
upon as an undertaking for old men. Sales-

manship is the one career that kindles the imaginations and genius of the young. It is a perfectly respectable career for one who has something valuable to sell.

We touch now on what is most dangerously
wrong in the moral incentives and tendencies
of the younger generation. Its one categorical
imperative, "Learn to sell yourself," means, being interpreted, "Get your value recognized by
society." Publicity managers, business psycho-
logists, sales-engineers, and their kind and
kindred, who are legion, have made the atmosphere of our times tense with pressures upon
every young person to get his value recognized.
If a new popular religion were founded to-
day, the first book of its gospel would undoubt-
edly treat of the psychology of salesmanship.
The spirit of this gospel has already invaded
the void left by the new universe constructed
with no "insides." The young person responds
with an intoxication, seldom sobered by any
consideration whatever of the really quite
primary questions whether he has any value,
and, if not, whether by dint of some old-fashioned exertion, he may acquire some. The
emphasis of the selling-slogan is, at least for a
young generation, off: it just misses the head of
the nail and strikes with a resounding whack

close beside it. Only the attentive notice that it is all noise with no honest drive.

The young person who is inspired to "sell" himself is encouraged by every pressure of his times to concern himself with only one thing, namely, "How to put it across." He hears on all sides that what he is to put across is of small consequence. He need not give himself much anxiety, if he is a teacher or preacher about what he is to teach or preach; nor, if he is a journalist or author or artist, about what he is to write or paint.

Efficiency in a universe of salesmen demands no special training or learning in any field whatever, save one—the technique of "touch." If you haven't the touch, you are "Out." If you have the "touch," you are "It." This technique is heaven's free gift to the happy mortal who is born "a good mixer," facile and suave in surface contacts. But it is also masterable by those unintrospective wits, who, wasting no time in meditating either their subject or their object, consider only their "objective," and therefore dedicate their days and their nights to the study of their public, their audience, their clientele.

Learned men in the universities are rapidly establishing the "technique of touch" on universal principles, applicable to all relations between the salesman and the public, from the marketing of short stories to transactions in gold brick. When this new science is perfected, it bids fair to displace ethics, logic, and the other elements of our bankrupt philosophy. For those who have acquired the new learning, those who have the "touch," prosper. They "get away with it." They "put it across."

Under the new system, success in life is felicitously described as "getting by." This modest expression indicates that our hero, though slightly elated by his efficiency, is no enthusiast. He is, on the contrary, just beneath his fine surface, a cynic. Knowing the hollowness of his interior, he does not respect himself. Suspecting that those with whom he traffics are equally hollow, he does not respect his public. His criterion of success implies acknowledgment that he is a fraud and his public a fool, who will pass him without challenge provided only that he "puts up a good front." It is understood that I am portraying one whom the "band-wagon" carries to the end of the road.

When I seek for an incarnate symbol of what the virtues of our young generation become when they are pushed to excess, I recall one of its representatives who burst upon us one summer evening in a crowded train coming out of

Washington. We were standing, some twenty of us, tired and hungry, jammed in the hot throat of the dining-car, waiting earnestly yet orderly for our turn at a seat. Just as one was vacated, in from the next coach dashed a youth of twenty-one, immaculate in white flannels, chin aloft and eyes hard ahead, like a picture drawn in the old days by Mr. C. D. Gibson for the late R. H. Davis. With a perfectly lordly gesture of the hand, as of one clearing the way for Rupert of Hentzau, and with a quiet but imperative "I beg your pardon," that handsome, that plausible, youth actually tried to break through the wedge of those twenty weary mortals and take that seat for himself. Shameful to relate, the wedge melted before him; he got by—almost to the head of the line, before an iron arm barred the passage, and a firm humorous voice exclaimed: "No, you don't, my boy! You'll have to work your way up, like the rest of us." Whereat that immaculate young importance, instantly collapsing, slunk and wriggled to the rear, while the twenty murmured to one another, "Where did he get that stuff?"

My illustrative personage, real and at the same time symbolical, obviously got his "stuff" from a society excessively dependent for its superiority upon car-makers, tailors, and books of etiquette. The morality of his period has worked upon my hero from without inward, but has not penetrated far. At the center, where the master should sit, there is a space without form and void. He has nothing, morally speaking, of his own. The time-spirit has clothed him in specious appearances. He travels upon credit which was accumulated in other days, when the Gibson chin was the outward sign of an inward determination. He is, therefore, in the figurative, and probably also in the literal, sense, "living beyond his means."

I will hazard a guess that at college he studied a "line," "worked off" his French, and attained in his studies a passing mark, which is now generally known as a "gentleman's grade." At the same time he lived softly in a palatial fraternity house contributed by over indulgent alumni, who themselves paid for their barracks accommodations in the old dormitory by tending furnaces, and the like. He had had his father's car at his disposal since his early 'teens. Naturally when he went to college, he required it still for transit from fraternity house to class room and for dances and week-end parties. Of course, if one has a good car, one must live up to one's car.

And so the Old Man, half in pity for his own austere youth, saw his son through in a style that he did not allow himself after a life-time of industry and thrift. "When my boy gets out in the world," the Old Man had said, "he'll have to shift for himself; but we'll give him a start with the best of them. Yes, sir, with the best of them!"

I will guess also that our young man is now in the employ of a corporation with very handsome offices, which gives him an apprentice's wage, sufficient to pay installments on his tailor's bill, while it authorizes an expense account allowing and encouraging him to enjoy the clubs, hotels, and costly little pleasures of big business men. All his life he has had unearned advantages thrust upon him; he takes them quite as a matter of course. He has always spent other people's money freely. Now it is a matter of duty to put on all the "side" that he can. He must eat and dress and drive in a fashion to "get in touch" with men whose income tax many times exceeds his income. Under the circumstances, it is altogether too soon to think of laying anything by. If he attempted that, he would have to "drop out of the running." He has, however, "invested" in an automobile, upholstered with the elegance of a parlor, and is asking his landlord to trust him for the last month's rent.

If he "puts it across" to a girl, formed on the same system—as I think he soon will—she, in her turn, will clutch at the "line" she has been taught. She will demand the right to be married without a ring, to retain her own name, to be secure from the expectation of children, to be allowed to pursue her own career, and to be guaranteed a "good time." To all of which demands he will yield ready assent. They will have a highly expensive engagement and a still more expensive wedding and honeymoon; and they will then attempt to "jolly things along" together.

They will find that they are unable to keep house comfortably in his upholstered car. He will discover that a modern establishment for two is, in spite of all that our grandmothers used to say, more difficult to swing than bachelor's quarters. It will appear that she is quite his equal as a spender. At first he may hope for some relief from the proceeds of that independent career which he has agreed to allow her to pursue. But he will learn very shortly that the kind of girl who stipulates for a marriage exempt from all the responsibilities of the traditional union becomes the kind of wife who puts all that she can lay hands on upon her own back, and yet leaves it more than half uncovered. She has been trained to dress and display herself for the kind of man that he is. But he is not quite equal to the task of maintaining the kind of a woman that she is. In two years or less, he will be single again and bankrupt—or an advertising manager on twenty thousand a year.

I add the alternative; because he may "get by." But a generation with a marked tendency towards the production and heroization of such figures and figurantes should beware of pressing its tendencies too far. "The gods creep up on feet of wool." A spending generation which trades on the moral and material accumulations of its predecessors, presently finds its stock exhausted. And though for a time, by its mastery of "touch" it may still sell water and market wind, in the long run it will not get by with that stuff.

V

THE SUPERIOR CLASS

Nothing is more deeply punished than the neglect of the affinities by which alone society should be formed, and the insane levity of choosing associates by others' eyes.

EMERSON.

That which takes my fancy most, in the heroic class, is the good humor and hilarity they exhibit.

EMERSON.

Great men are thus a collyrium to clear our eyes from egotism, and enable us to see other people and their works.

EMERSON.

THE SUPERIOR CLASS

Every one who reflects concludes that the welfare of society depends upon its management by superior persons. The thoughtful democrat does not object to hereditary aristocracies because they perpetuate the management of superior persons. He objects because in the long run they allow unenergetic incompetents to remain in office and manage, while able men cool their shins in the corridor. In sixteenth century England, when knighthood was still in late autumnal flower, an aristocratic author maintained, apparently with full conviction, that one of noble blood sits his horse and conducts himself in all manly exercises with a grace beyond the reach of the common man. But in the seventeenth century it appears that the noble blood had ceased to transmit its virtues; for a writer on etiquette of that period warns gentlemen that they should never enter any athletic competition with yokels unless they are sure that they can excel. From that time on, the hereditary principle began to be supplanted by another method for attaining the same indispensable object.

Democracy, politically or socially considered, is a method of recruiting a superior class. To this end democracy institutes a kind of Olympic contest, inviting all who think themselves athletes to contend for renown. The moment one regards the matter in this light it becomes manifestly absurd to say because democracy admits all comers to her contests that she has no standards. The theory is, on the contrary, that precisely because she admits all comers she can put her standards very high. Two sects of unbelievers chiefly oppose and attempt to thwart her central purpose: First, those who wish the hurdles lowered and the pace slowed so that all who enter may cross the tape together. Second, those who, reviving the abrogated hereditary principle, seek to disqualify new competitors by the introduction of standards irrelevant to the object of the competition, as if one should say, "No one may enter the Marathon who does not pronounce his final r's as they do on Commonwealth Avenue."

With the rapidly enlarging feminine influence in American life certain questions are thrust upon the student of democracy. Will women, as they have promised, raise our essential standards? Will they constitute an effective increment to the superior class? Or will their long enjoyment of "special privilege" render difficult an adjustment to their mere "rights?" Will they have the courage to contend on really equal terms for a share in the social estate which democracy is ever bent upon repartitioning, or will they warily intrigue for the disqualification of all contestants who are not of a certified "gigmanity"?

My own observation is that in the modern woman much more distinctly than in the modern man a bold imagination is still ineffectually struggling with a timorous intelligence. This is particularly true of those women in the "sheltered class," who are grouped by a writer in the *New York Times* with the Southern peasantry and the Northern foreign-born as requiring an education for the ballot. Not wishing to dogmatize, an objectionable and irritating masculine habit, I will take an illustrative case. I will take the case of a writer of talent, Mrs. Katherine Fullerton Gerould, who has distinguished herself both as a skilful concocter of the American short story, which we are told is the best in the world, and as a producer of critical essays of a remarkable tartness, dealing with men, manners, morals, and religion. In her fiction, imagination has the victory; in her essays, the timorous intelligence. To turn from the fiction to the essays affords a contrast as beguiling as to watch an agile performer on the stage who appears at one moment as a Long John Silver, walks behind a screen, and reappears a moment later as Lydia Languish.

As a writer of short stories Mrs. Gerould plays the part of a man in a world of men with fine bravado, only occasionally reminding one of Rosalind's remark, that doublet and hose must show itself courageous to petticoat. She owes something of her outfit to Mrs. Wharton, something to Henry James, and perhaps still more to Mr. Kipling of the Indian tales. A half-dozen of her best performances—for examples, "Vain Oblations," "The Miracle," "Wesendonck," and "The Weaker Vessel"— are as good as anybody's, originally conceived and brilliantly executed. They have taken shape in an emancipated and unabashed imagination, which constructs moral predicaments of high tension and probes with merciless artistic delight into possibilities that are sometimes to the last degree horrid and indeed almost insufferably revolting. Her studiously nonchalant manner enhances the effect of her matter. She presents the discoveries of her imagination with firm objectivity in a style terse, elliptical, mannish, like a travelled clubman back from the heart of Africa relating his adventures to other clubmen who have also been in Africa. Her book on Hawaii is written without this literary mask and contains, as I remember, a sigh or so in the character of Rosalind. Yet venturous curiosity is the dominant note; and one feels, when reading the account of the leper colony and the orgiastic native dances, that the author, like many highly refined ladies, might be prevailed upon, if properly chaperoned, to join a Senegalese headhunt, as a spectator, or to knit a scarf, like Dickens's French women, at the foot of a revolutionary place of justice.

Then the bold teller of tales disappears behind the screen to reappear in her recent volume of essays, *Modes and Morals,* as an excessively feminine "particular person" with a soul formed on old mahogany and blue china, with a rather vacuous, old-fashioned New Englandish cant about "high-thinking" and "intellectual values," with an obviously sincere attachment to parlormaids and "nice things," and with an overwhelming fear that in the widening social democracy of these times some bounder who says "don't" for "doesn't" may leap the barrier inclosing those who say "doesn't" and dine with a friend or relative in the superior class—with possible matrimonial consequences quite too dreadful to contemplate. I have only begun in this long sentence to enumerate Mrs. Gerould's trepidations. She fears the world she lives in and pretty much all its works and ways. Her fundamental and controlling fear is due to "the increased hold of the democratic fallacy on the public mind." She fears materialism. She has also a great horror of science. She is afraid of new races and the influx of an inferior population which will basely compromise with mission furniture and domestic rugs. She apprehends that these forces will extirpate something precious which she calls "culture."

I relish, as I have intimated, the style and the æsthetically applied splashes of barbaric color in her stories. No one paints better than she the beautiful wife in one of our best families, pacing restlessly across a Chinese rug under tall windows through floods of glowing sunlight, meditating an elopement, but restrained by those delicacies of feeling which, as every one knows, are developed by living amid priceless old Chippendale. I enjoy so much the bravado of her stories that I hesitate to say how deeply I have been shocked by the pusillanimity of her

essays and by the moral and intellectual bank-
ruptcy of the class to which they are presumably
designed to bring comfort and aid.

So far as I am concerned, however, the offence has been committed, and I am willing, if
it is possible, to turn my discomfiture to some
public profit. "By suffering we learn," says the
Greek dramatist; and out of our suffering, one
may add, we teach. I happen to be interested in
public instruction, being associated with one of
those State universities which, as many of us believe, are in a fair way to fufill to the people the
promises which Jefferson, Franklin, and Lincoln saw in American life. Let the general
reader fancy, then, my embarrassment when I
found Mrs. Gerould declaring with emphasis
that in the matter of education "we cannot count
on the West to help us, for the West is cursed
with State universities." Mrs. Gerould cannot,
of course, have intended any incivility here.
She is a writer of the most correct taste and
complete decorum. The fault was, in a sense,
my own, for I had—inadvertently, to be sure—
intruded upon, or, as we sometimes say in our
brutal Western fashion, "butted into," a kind of
boudoir chat of the author with her confidential
friends. And yet I cannot help feeling—it is a

palliative to my mortification—that Mrs. Gerould was in some slight degree responsible for my unhappy gaucherie. She might, so to speak, have taken the precaution of drawing the curtains and closing the door.

Embarrassed as I was by overhearing her confidential opinions of the West and its universities, I was even more acutely perturbed by another matter. I felt quite indecently out of place and ruddy with shame at having thrust myself into the private circle to which alone she must have desired to communicate her views of Miss Alcott's New England and the culture of Concord. Like many Americans, whether still dwelling in adorable nooks where their ancestors settled two hundred years ago, or whethei scattered across the plains or among the Sierras or up and down the Sacramento and San Joaquin valleys, I feel a mysterious and almost passionate tenderness for New England. Wherever the sons and daughters of her spirit may sojourn or wander New England still pulls at their hearts as their motherland. With her exquisite white villages, clustering around the white church spire, under the maples and the pure blue heaven, between overshadowing hills, she flashes upon the inward eye, in smoky city

or southwestern desert, as a vision of home—
the historic home.

There rest from their labors seven or eight
generations of simple, pious folk, who, toiling
from sunrise to sunset, brought the forlorn hope
of their time to reluctant blossom and explored
the difficult meaning of a new world—small independent farmers who lived on the land,
skilled workmen who did not watch the clock,
the doctor who cared more for his patient than
for his fee, and the minister passing rich on
six hundred dollars a year.

For one reason or another these provincial
folk—it must be remembered that the Adamses
now declare even Boston provincial—these provincial folk, as all our fashionable anti-Puritan
writers are complaining, showed a marked indifference to the more expensive pleasures of
the senses. I sometimes gravely doubt whether
it is true, as is often asserted, that they did not
care for beauty. They had, for example, a kind
of native instinct for beautiful and sound wood-
work. Urbane people of more taste than means
are still combing the clocks, highboys, and side-
boards out of the remoter hill villages of New
England. Still it probably is true that they gave
comparatively little attention to the decoration
of their homes or to the adornment of their

persons. By virtue or by necessity they dispensed with silk next the skin and with many other things soft, bright, and luxurious which a really nice person to-day can hardly do without. If one does without them one ceases, as Mrs. Gerould intimates, to be nice. The cost of being nice is going up. Thence the shadow of dread which overspreads us. Thence our present misery. Few of us are able to keep our bodies in the style to which our imaginations are accustomed.

With New Englanders of the older culture the case was different. Perhaps nature meant more to them and manufactured articles less. Perhaps the fine, clear air of their Doric villages, and beauty that walks abroad in their mountains and runs down their brooks and breaks like a dryad, an incarnate Spring, from the bark of their white birches in April—perhaps this order of beauty in 1840 more fully slaked the thirst of the soul than it does nowadays. Perhaps in 1840 a philosopher living by Walden Pond on thirty dollars a year really found beauty of a sort in a plain and sound integrity within. Perhaps Alcott and Thoreau and Emerson did actually value high thinking and veritably did rate their daily conversation with Plato, Hafiz, and Confucius above tea-

table gossip. Miss Alcott's New England remains precious to us and Concord is still a
sacred place in the memory, because there the
people who talked about "intellectual values"
meant what they were saying. When they renounced "high living" they renounced it for
themselves, and not merely for tradespeople and
artisans.

But now comes Mrs. Gerould and, having
reread Miss Alcott's books in the light of our
new and modern culture, intimates that it
doesn't much matter what these people meant,
since they were outside the pale, since they were,
in fact, "underbred." In the first place, they
were too poor to be otherwise. Secondly,
"breeding," as such, is simply not a product of
the independent village. The "friends of Emerson," she declares, lacked the gift of "civilized
contacts." Thirdly, they said "don't" for
"doesn't" and neglected the subjunctive mood.
Fourthly, their parties were not properly chaperoned. Fifthly, their scholarliness was
"bigoted" and they exhibited an underbred interest in education, such as, Mrs. Gerould sup-
poses, can be matched to-day "only in the
Middle West." Sixthly, they were "blatantly
moral"—a really nice person in our day may
be religious, but to be moral is a little quaint.

Seventhly, they showed their underbreeding by their patriotism—a coarse note. Eighthly, their dress, household service, and furniture were bad, and, what was infinitely worse, "they did not know it." Really nice people to-day live and have their being in a consciousness of their furniture, their household service, and their dress. Ninthly, and lastly, and most confidentially, "you really would not want to spend a week in the house of any one of them."

This bill of indictment was clearly intended for the ears of a superior class or a coterie superior to the Emersonian circle. We aristocrats, suggests Mrs. Gerould, must make a stand for culture; we must get together and exclude both the dead and the living whose furniture does not come up to our standards and who have not mastered the subjunctive mood. Now, to take this line is going to hurt Mrs. Gerould's popularity with the great majority who have not heard of the subjunctive. It is going to have a very estranging effect upon the masses of Americans who still cling to fumed oak. This is of no consequence to her. She definitely and defiantly announces that she wishes to draw apart, that her faith and her fun depend upon the preservation of "caste and class and clan." But it is of consequence to a major democratic interest which all sorts of common people have at heart. It is of interest to the cause of culture, which is in danger of being mortally wounded in the house of its professed friends. Mrs. Gerould injures the cause of culture by identifying it with social superciliousness and by representing it as something to be made a clan monopoly. She injures its reputation still more by an extraordinary overemphasis of external advantages which a thief may carry off in the night and by an equally extraordinary neglect of those internal advantages which are as inaccessible to the thief as the love of God.

In the New Jerusalem every woman of culture, perhaps,—every really nice woman—will have a huddle of colored servants on the stairs of her mansion and well-trained parlormaids hovering in the halls, dusting the Chinese Chippendale, cleaning the Bokhara rugs, and opening the door to the members of the superior class. But in this world a good many women of culture will continue to prove their amenity, as they have always done, primarily by more strictly personal graces of mind and heart. Among these graces not least is the gift of not seeing what ought not to be seen. I should suppose that, in the presence of Miss Alcott's courage and gayety, a really opulent culture might have thrown a cloak of invisibility, which is much like the cloak of charity, over that dress of hers, which would otherwise remind us that she made it herself and none too well.

But a culture which goes deep as the heart has a certain "levelling" and democratical tendency. Therefore Mrs. Gerould declares with a bang that "culture is not a democratic achievement, because culture is inherently snobbish." She believes in the thing—it becomes a thing by her definitions—but she also believes that there is not enough of the thing to go around. Accordingly, she trusts that the numbers of those who aspire to it will be kept down. She says that she pins her hope of effective restriction on the older Eastern universities and the choice minority. Apparently they are to coöperate with her in reducing the wages of the skilled workman, who is now beginning to be able to send his son to one of the accursed State universities and to provide for his family some of the external means of grace the lack of which made the Alcotts so "underbred." Since the majority will not value a minority engaged in closing the door in its face, she insists that the minority must unite to value itself. Clearly such a minority as she contemplates can have no value but to itself.   Here is "aristocracy" in the last despairing gasps of self-consumption.

Emerson and Matthew Arnold in their day were often thought to be "tainted with aristocratic principles."   But place their idea of culture beside Mrs. Gerould's and instantly you would take those prophets for demagogues, flatterers of the "rascal many."   They were not, at any rate, afraid of their world.   And they did not pretend that what they prescribed for the superior class would destroy the multitude. Culture they conceived of as the steadily strengthening bond between man and man in an ever larger and larger company able to satisfy its standards.   For they conceived of culture not as a thing, but as an enlightened and enlightening spirit, a spirit of wide embrace, exacting in its discipline, but like the great historic Church of Christendom, of catholic and charitable imagination, eager to enfold a converted world and, so, eminently adapted to the democratic societies of the future.

It is thirty years since I read Miss Alcott's stories and I doubt whether I should enjoy them now as much as I enjoy Mrs. Gerould's. But there is a charm in certain pages of her *Journal,* an "amenity," of an order which I seek in vain in the far more clever works of her suc-

cessor to my admiration. When Bronson Alcott, returning from his western lecturing tour,
presented himself late at night to his poverty
stricken family, they flew down the stairs, wife
and four girls, in their night wear, to meet him.
(A well-bred person would, of course, have sent
one of her huddle of colored servants.) The
philosopher presented himself somewhat apol-
ogetically, confessing that he had lost his over-
coat and that his net profits had amounted to
only one dollar. Mrs. Alcott, that underbred
woman, kissed the old sage affectionately and
said: "I think you did very well indeed, dear."
And they all trooped up to bed—heaven knows
how many of them to a room, covered with
heaven knows what a horror of a carpet.

Now, that domestic scene contrasts rather
shabbily, I admit, with Mrs. Gerould's picture
of a really nice woman meditating a fracture
of the seventh commandment in a spacious sun-
flooded chamber with a Chinese rug. Morals
change with modes. As Mrs. Gerould has
taught us, "civilization means accepting nicer
and nicer things and rejecting nasty ones." And
so I shall probably continue to read Mrs. Gerould's stories and to neglect Miss Alcott's, and
yet to feel, after all, that though the later writer
is undeniably more chic, the earlier one may

have had a finer organ for detecting those "majestical traits," those flashes of the grand style in common men and women everywhere, which Emerson truly says are the charm and wonder of time.

VI

EDUCATION BY THE PEOPLE

It is time that villages were universities, and their elder inhabitants the fellows of universities, with leisure—if they are indeed so well off—to pursue liberal studies the rest of their lives.

THOREAU.

If any beggar for a church school oppose a local tax for schools or a higher school tax, take him to the huts of the forgotten women and children, and in their hopeless presence remind him that the church system of education has not touched tens of thousands of these lives and ask him whether he thinks it wrong that the commonwealth should educate them.

WALTER HINES PAGE.

I believe in the perpetual regeneration of society, and in the immortality of democracy and in growth everlasting.

WALTER HINES PAGE.

EDUCATION BY THE PEOPLE

"Hitherto she but plows and hammers," wrote Carlyle of America in 1850. And he was only repeating and summing up the prejudices of innumerable English travellers who had inspected our civilization when he added this painful tribute to the American cousins: "They have begotten, with a rapidity beyond recorded example, eighteen millions of the greatest bores ever seen in the world before,— that hitherto is their feat in History." That was spoken, as Malvolio says, without much "mitigation or remorse of voice." Yet the American "bore" of 1850, believing still, in spite of *himself,* in democratic institutions might have heartened his faith by a retrospect over the history of anti-American prophecy. If he had run through a shelf full of the books of travel in the United States written by apprehensive English Tories, he would have observed that the hostile critics of democracy had already shifted their ground. In the earlier years, they prophesied against our political constitution, confidently predicting that a government by the people could not be permanently established. When, even before the Civil War, a reasonable degree of stability seemed to be attained, they prophesied against our society, proclaiming on many a caustic page, that, though the people had accomplished what they set out to perform, they were not to be congratulated on their achievement. Popular government, they conceded, might endure, but only to perpetuate a society of shopkeepers who would employ Reading, 'Riting, and 'Rithmetic merely to put money in their purses. For the "bore" of 1850 there was an escape from this humdrum prospect by the door of humility and by the secret passages of hope. Prophecy had failed once and might be wrong again. *He* might not be the fulfillment but only the pioneer of the democratic dream. For him, the plow and hammer; for his sons, the pursuit of happiness.

Perhaps the most encouraging thing about an American is that he never accepts what other people tell him is his destiny. Cherishing we scarcely know what enkindling vision, dim or distinct, the American of those middle years turned in the thick of his business and in the confusion of internal strife to the perfecting of his system of popular education—his second great democratic experiment. Upon his common schools he had built high schools, and upon his high schools, he was now beginning to build his State universities—all dedicated to the proposition that democracy opens all legitimate paths of opportunity to all her people. What grounds there were for predicting that educational institutions so constituted and so dedicated must perish from the earth, one may discover by studying the half-dozen preliminary, perfunctory and unread pages entitled "History," which appear as the first chapter in the fat, prosperous-looking catalogues of the great State universities of the West.

Established these institutions are beyond the shadow of a doubt. And those whose profession and pleasure it is to prophesy against the people have advanced now to the second stage of adverse criticism. "We admit," they say, "that you flourish—'like the green bay tree.' But what, after all, has education by the people accomplished? Does not your 'second great democratic experiment' confirm the results of your first? What has come of your effort to lift yourself out of the forge and the furrow by your bootstraps? Do you not still plow and hammer? You have put money in your purse. But

where, O Demos, are your spiritual rents?
What commerce have you with the skies? Has
not this your supereminent organ of popular
education, the State University, for its being's
end and aim the multiplication of the father's
material goods by the son? And must it not be
so in the nature of things forever?"

It is not difficult to understand how, warrant-
ably or not, the notion spreads abroad that the
State university, with its prominent technical
schools and colleges, is in the grip of a "carnal"
imagination, and that, through its intimate intercourse with the people, it exerts an immense
influence tending to fortify the people in their
besetting sin, in their natural materialism.
Such is the penalty for leading a public life.
The State institution, like a representative in
Congress, gets into power by promising to look
after the interests of its constituents, or rather,
perhaps, like a promoter, it promises big returns on money invested. What is worse, it
pays the returns it has promised. Now the
frank parleying with the people incident to the
gaining of popular support; the discussion of
higher education and the profits of research
with chambers of commerce and clubs of
Rotarians; the unblushing western way of meeting in legislatures and voting to pass the hat

for contributions all through the state—these vulgar methods offend to the quick the sensibilities of men who studied ethics and learned to despise the dollar on foundations provided by benevolent corporation lawyers, and reclaimed banditti of high finance. "You send us your boy from the counter or the shop or the plow-tail," so runs the argument to the parent, "and in four years we will return him to you with tripled or quadrupled earning capacity." "You sow ten bushels of scientific investigation, and you will reap a thousand bushels of improvement." "Every cent put into technical research will increase and multiply, and, sooner or later, will come clinking back into your pocket as silver and gold." Irresistible! this appeal to the pocket. "But," says the Idealist, "is not this to join forces with the ominously popular journalism and that eloquent advertising which day and night in America burn incense before the Golden Calf? How in any way does this type of 'higher education' assist in giving the naturally sensual passions of a democracy a bias towards the stars?"

Merited and timely as such criticism may appear to a transient observer of the State university, it is recognized as superficial and essentially false by all those who have felt the inner throb and glow of the enterprise. Idealist the institution is not, if idealism means a sterile yearning for the unattainable. Materialist it is not, if materialism is identified with satisfaction in the welfare of the senses. The State university to-day is at the same time intensely visionary and intensely practical: its driving power is the creative artist's desire to externalize and eternize his dream. With eyes fixed upon that end, it does not shrink from the coarse tasks of mixing pigments, quarrying stone, or melting bronze. It would honor every truth by use, and it holds that the triumph of the spiritual is the subjugation of the material. The financial support which it solicits is the means to the realization of a vision embracing almost the whole of life, and the wealth which it helps to create is but the first fruits of its contemplated harvest.

Not the only fruit. An idealist from the University of Edinburgh says that if you are to be governed by the people, you must submit to "collective folly." A realist from a State university says that if you are to be governed by the people, you had better educate your governors. An idealist from the University of Oxford, demands a wise paternal government, providing for all its children in their ignorance and distress. A realist from a State university declares that a wise and truly paternal government, prevents the distress and ignorance of its children by showing them how to provide for themselves.

But still another Oxford graduate tells us that the remedy for the "evils of democracy" is to strengthen the power of the State by making it the central organ for the dissemination of the best that has been said and thought in the world. These words the Faculty of a State university would probably recognize as fairly descriptive of their undertaking. They would dignify the entire range of human conduct by discovering for all the people, and by making prevail from the lowest to the loftiest, the right and excellent form of every activity. They resent with justice the prevalent notion that the love of light is a monopoly in possession of the old New England colleges. "Even in our concern for the applied sciences," they say, "there operates the identical passion for perfection which you extol and strive to keep unspotted from the world. You have preserved your idealism in glass jars; we have not lost ours by putting it to work in the bread of life. Immersed in sense though we seem to be, we are Platonists no less than you, pursuing through the things that lie nearest us the divine idea, and we shall pass in due time from the love of sensuous to the love of supersensuous beauty."

"Will you? That is precisely the question," rejoins a skeptical voice from somewhere east of Buffalo. "Go and communicate to the farmers your passion for sweetness and light! In all seriousness, are you approaching the possibility of doing that? Does that possibility lie in the line of your march? We do not doubt your ability to pass from triumph to triumph in your conquest of the material world, and indefinitely to improve your technical processes and increase your economic efficiency. Yet to us your absorption in agriculture, business, and engineering does not seem to prophesy a new generation of more genial, humane, and conversable men but a second generation of Carlyle's 'bores,' speeding on safer railroads through richer fields to bigger business, and sitting down of an evening in more admirably constructed dwellings, better heated, better plumbed, and better lighted, to read the stock quotations and meditate more profitable investments. We do not see the provision in your scheme of higher education for shunting the people to a line of progress issuing in a society that is an end in itself. We do not see at what point you are going to be able to send your campaigners through the granges with the message that the wealth of the State is not in its soil but in its cultivated men and women. When do you expect to go before your legislators and get them to appropriate a million dollars for a kind of education that cannot be guaranteed to return a penny to the pockets of the tax-payers? When they are ready to do that, we will agree that you are equipped to compete with New England colleges which carry on the great human traditions. Till they are ready to do that, the point of departure for our higher education will remain the terminus of yours. Whatever your secret aspirations toward a genuine intellectual leadership may be, you cannot flee from the destiny of democratic enterprises. The 'beast with many heads' can go only where his feet will carry him—and we know his trough, well enough."

Though these charges against education by the people are serious enough, eastern critics of the State university are not content with pointing out that its character is determined and its functions limited by its financial dependence upon the tax-payers. If this were the only controlling factor, they say, some modest provision for the higher cultivation of the mind might be lugged shamefacedly through the legislature, clinging to the skirts of a magnificent provision for the higher cultivation of the fields. And so, indeed, the university administration does maintain on its own demesnes a little ground room for the humanities just as the game commission preserves among the corn a little refuge for the prairie chickens, as a barely tolerated relic of feudal privileges. But, argue the critics, the immediate determination of the educational character of the State university is by the high schools and the stress of their influence is in precisely the same direction as that of the taxpayers.

This is again to attack the democratic principle and to deny the power of the State university to exercise any high intellectual leadership. If it were in fact and in theory the head of the system of public education, then, one might admit it need not depair of its longest hopes and its most ambitious dreams, despite the indifference of the tax-payers. Actually empowered with their will, entrusted with their educational destiny, it would think for itself and for all its members, bring its subordinate parts into harmony with its great design, set its own high standards of excellence, and see to it that no good securable by private means should be unpurchasable by the colossal purse of the people. These, however, as we are informed, are idle and unprofitable speculations. The hard fact, which sooner or later must be faced, is that the State university has no independent life nor in the last analysis any important originating power. The body of which it is theoretically the head will not endure its dictation. The high schools dictate to the University, the parents dictate to the high schools, the children dictate to the parents; the parents comply with the children, the high schools comply with the parents, the university complies with the high schools. It is outvoted.

The high schools, thus runs the argument, are frankly not interested in higher education but in assisting a miscellaneous constituency by a short route to a livelihood. They assert that the number of their pupils who will later enter the university is so small as to be negligible in planning their curriculum. Yet coupled with the definite understanding that the high school graduate has not been intentionally prepared for anything but "practical life" is the equally definite understanding that the possession of a high school diploma qualifies him for admission to the university. The sheer necessity of accepting what the high school offers has caused the university helplessly to acquiesce in the strange new theory that one subject is as good as another.

Now, to those in the State university who are concerned with the older "academic" studies which lead through a long preliminary discipline of the taste and a gradual opening of the understanding to the employment and use of our "intellectual heritage"—to those concerned with such studies this new educational doctrine is a rank heresy, begotten in confusion, and repugnant to experience and common sense. To accept it is to assume that in four years you can make a bachelor of arts of a man who, for instance, can neither write, read, nor speak any language under the sun. "That," say the critics, "is exactly what the liberal arts college in the State university is trying to do, and the undertaking is preposterous. Why not abandon it and accept the manifest destiny of a 'free' institution? For there is apparently a kind of higher education which does not rest upon anything lower. Your brethren who profess the useful arts and the applied sciences seem to thrive on your heresy. They have adapted themselves to their environment. We prophesy that they will prove the fittest to survive the struggle for existence. We prophesy that, so far as your power to support them is concerned, the humanities are doomed."

Interested observers situated in endowed institutions in the East have reflected upon this position of affairs with something like self-congratulation. When the young prospering universities of the West first began to make their as yet undefined influence felt far beyond the boundaries of their States, it was feared in some quarters that they would cut into the constituency and menace the prestige of their ever venerable elders. But now, if we may credit Professor Morris of Yale, the danger has pretty well blown over.* The State institutions have attained their majority, their character is settled, and the bent they have taken puts them out of the competition. "Their arts course," he says, "has been comparatively unimportant"—it will be noted that the rest of the sentence subtly yet significantly serves to define "unimportant"— "hardly more than another college in addition to those already existing in the State." A handsome compliment, either way you look at it! Their only considerable function, he adds in effect, is vocational training; and, in performing that, they supplement, not supplant, the function of their academic predecessors, which

* *Yale Review,* April, 1913.

still, as of old, is, "to put the young man between eighteen and twenty-two into possession
of his intellectual heritage, to hand on to him
the wealth of emotion and experience which the
race has accumulated." We may therefore now
amicably divide the educational world—I give
the gist of his conclusions in my own words.
Since a complex of forces, largely economic, has
inevitably locked the State university and the
high school in one system, and the endowed college and the expensive preparatory school in
another, the Western university will look after
the body and the eastern college will look after
the soul. And we are sure that this arrangement ought to be agreeable to all parties concerned.

Such a partition of functions, however, the
western State university can ill afford to regard
with complacency. For what would the permanent acceptance of the intellectual hegemony
of the eastern colleges involve and what would
it signify? It would involve either sacrificing
whatever youths of high intellectual promise
the West could produce to its soulless vocational system, or else sending them eastward at
the age of fourteen, for school and college, with
the probability that they would lose contact
and sympathy with their early surroundings,

and a fair likelihood that they would form their connexions and make their residence in the East. It would tend, in other words, to remove the leaven from the inert lump and place it in the risen bread—to strengthen the lust for stocks and bonds that prevails everywhere in Chicago and the love for sweetness and light that prevails everywhere in New York. It would signify that the supposedly opulent West was too poor, to crude, too busy, too blind, too much bent upon improving its plows and hammers to give any attention to creating a refined society, to offering any satisfaction to the needs of the spirit, to affording any shelter for those of its children who hunger and thirst for the "accumulated emotion and experience of the race." If it be true, that to such young persons the western institution can now offer little or no high guidance or stimulating companionship, it should seem to be their part of discretion to depart from it and the part of wisdom for the State university with all haste to take measures to prevent their departure. Preaching resignation to them that sit in darkness is a new rôle for the children of light.

There is something, furthermore, in these deductions which should make an ordinary American, without reference to sectional interests, open his eyes and consider what to do next. For it is to be observed that the people as educators are to acquiesce not merely in an eastern college monopoly in the production of liberal culture but also in a class monopoly in the consumption of it, entrenched, fortified, and established by hereditary wealth. It has been a popular superstition among us that the power of great fortunes in a small class is offset by the power of great ideas in a large class. We have hitherto regarded the facility with which a young man of slender means could enter with natural gifts upon his intellectual heritage as perpetually guaranteeing free competition for the possession of the things of the mind. We now learn that in the immediate future the intellectual heritage is to be reserved more and more exclusively for the rich man's son and added to his other advantages. For only he can afford the costly luxury of a secondary school which *prepares*. The pupils of the high school, says our author, "often young men of character and capacity, are not prepared for academic study and can be admitted only at the price of the retardation of the intellectual advance of the college." This amounts to saying that our public schools, which we had thought opened the doors to the highest educational opportunities, are become, on the contrary, a perpetual bar to those opportunities. Professor Morris is entirely candid in this matter; one should be grateful to him for putting the case in so clear a light. "The democratic ideal," he says, "and the intellectual ideal are here in conflict"!

From this statement one infers, however, that he is not especially intimate with "the democratic ideal." Education of the people, by the people, for the people—does that not include provision for the liberal culture of the people? Because Democracy has borne heavy burdens and the heat of the day and her children are many, are we to conclude that the light has faded from her eyes, that her strength is spent, her heart grown dull and indifferent to her "young men of promise and capacity?" Because the mighty Mother has not wholly accomplished in the twinkling of an eye what has hitherto been the slow work of centuries, shall we charge her with imperfect vision, abandon our faith in her, declare her incapable of providing for her offspring? In the watches of the night she takes counsel of her tragic history and the days still fresh in memeory when friend and foe alike pointed to the irreconcilable conflict between her democratic ideal and black slavery. She recalls that in that hour some of her counsellors saw no solution of her difficulties but to divide the continent into a democracy of the North and a slaveocracy of the South, just as now it is proposed to divide it into a giant working materialism of the West and a leisurely affluent idealism of the East. And she remembers in what throes of emancipative anguish she preserved her integrity and realized her dream. Is there none of that faith left?

To those who know the temper of the State universities and their friends it is absurd to suggest that they should entertain any such proposals for sectional peace and territorial distribution as I have been reviewing. Their battle is already more than half won, and they are exultant with the prospect of complete victory. They have shown to the people the folly and the turpitude of wasting the sweet uses of time in indolent expectation of unmerited opportunities and unearned benefits—of waiting for what they want and for what is within their own power to command till some prince of special privilege in his genial hour shall see fit to give it to them. They have taught the people to extend into the field of higher education the great elementary virtue of standing on their own feet and paying their own way. They have demonstrated the people's ability to obtain what they desire; it only remains to kindle their imagination with a vision of what they lack. Articles like that of our Eastern critic are dropping the necessary spark.

It is absurd to assert that great commonwealths of two to six million inhabitants cannot, in providing centres for the higher learning, compete successfully with the sporadic generosity of a few scores of private individuals. It is absurd to declare that a great commonwealth cannot afford to maintain in its university a liberal arts college of absolutely the first class, and within its own high school system ample and thorough preparation of its superior young men and women for entrance upon university studies. In the brutal tongue of the market, a high grade professor of philosophy or of classical philology is not a dearer commodity than a high grade professor of civil engineering or of soil fertility. The higher and the lower technical education which has already been provided is not less but more costly than equivalent provision for the so-called "humanities."

But to come to the heart of the whole matter, it is equally absurd to declare that the support of the people—the theoretical and applied approbation of the average man—cannot be organized except for material interests and self-regarding ends. In the humblest strata of society, as history blazons, it has been organized again and again for the adoration of God and the recovery of the Holy Sepulchre. Critics who sneer at the desires of the people simply do not understand the desires of the people. They do not perceive what to the candid eye is the most obvious fact in human history, namely, that the "vulgar herd," lost man everywhere and in all times, is struggling blindly, confusedly, hungrily to find his way back to that lost Eden which haunts the human heart. When the "vulgar herd" believed that theology had the best clue to the land of their heart's desire, they built the mediaeval cathedrals. When they began to suspect that the clue lies elsewhere, they established the State universities.

Church and State, we are accustomed to say, have in this country no interdependence; and ignorant persons conclude and declare that the State university is necessarily irreligious. It is a capital error. No one who reads his national annals with any attention can fail to perceive that religion is indissociably knit with the State, recognized in its courts, its senate chambers, its polling places, its public documents, its oaths of office, and, with more splendor in the language of its constitution and in official utterance of its great public servants. An invisible Majesty is invoked by the religion of the State to bind its citizens to truth, justice, and domestic tranquillity, and to fortify them in their resolution to transmit unimpaired to succeeding generations their civil and political and religious liberties. A university of the State, as a central organ of its life, is unfaithful to its trust if it does not uphold this religion.

Now the very obligation to refrain from denominational religious instruction which the State universities are under should make it appear the more imperatively their duty to bring not some but all of their students into quickening relationship with those purely human traditions which preserve through secular ages a regard for beauty, wisdom, temperance, truth, justice, and magnanimity. In the secular ages these traditions are perpetuated in great part by the study of what used to be called "humane letters," and the virtues and powers developed by this study are the flowering in character of what used to be called "liberal culture." With these objects of liberal culture the democratic practice has been blindly and heedlessly in conflict, at times; the democratic ideal, never. And one may venture confidently to predict that if the present organization of public education is inimical to them, if free access to them is menaced by an exclusive linking of the endowed colleges with the expensive preparatory schools, then the people through their State universities will be touched in their deepest impulses to reassert their interest in them, will be inspired by their highest hopes to reopen popular access to them, and will not cease to provide for them till they have proved their equality of devotion to them with the oldest colleges in the land.

VII
VOCATION

A man is like a bit of Labrador spar, which has no lustre as you turn it in your hand, until you come to a particular angle; then it shows deep and beautiful colors. There is no adaptation or universal applicability in men, but each has his special talent, and the mastery of successful men consists in adroitly keeping themselves where and when that turn shall be oftenest to be practised.

EMERSON.

If he thinks a sonnet the flower and result of the world, let him sacrifice all to the sonnet.

EMERSON.

I read in the Gulistan, or Flower Garden, of Sheik Sadi of Shiraz, that "They asked a wise man, saying: Of the many celebrated trees which the Most High God has created lofty and umbrageous, they call none azad, or free, excepting the cypress, which bears no fruit; what mystery is there in this? He replied: Each has its appropriate produce, and appointed season, during the continuance of which it is fresh and blooming, and during their absence dry and withered; to neither of which states is the cypress exposed, being always flourishing; and of this nature are the azads."

THOREAU.

*It is not to diffuse you that you were born of your mother and father
 —it is to identify you;
It is not that you should be undecided, but that you should be
 decided;
Something long preparing and formless is arrived and formed in you.*

WHITMAN.

VOCATION

"That maleficent word 'service'!" exclaims a critic for whom I have high respect, and tears the word from his lexicon. The cry is a protest against the disparagement of the contemplative life by the champions of the active life. Since at the present time the "practical" men display the arrogance engendered by an overwhelming predominance, I sympathize with the spirit of the protest. And yet the moment that one sets to work to justify the protest, one finds oneself in need precisely of that discarded word "service." For either one must admit that the contemplative life is indefensible or one must contend that the contemplative life is serviceable.

Words which have long exhibited a radiant energy, words and things like "God," "patriotism," "home," and "pure gold" are not to be lightly rejected in periods like our own, when their magic has fallen into temporary abeyance or when their value has suffered from mishandling. Before we abandon them to accept some wretched modern substitute—a band of greyish-white platinum, thin and fragile, for a plain ring of pure gold or "a stream of tendency" for "God"—we had better scrape the encrustations of time and base uses from the old symbols, and see whether a divine fire does not still burn at the heart of them.

Before we finally make up our minds to scoff at the whole idea of service, we had better scrutinize it rather carefully in relation to the whole idea contained in the word "vocation," which survives in the maligned phrase "vocational training." Whenever educators assemble, they begin to consult anxiously together on what can be done to impart a loftier tone and keener incentives to higher education. On such an occasion, after several of us had proposed the customary modern mechanical means of "raising the standards," a university president remarked with a kind of apologetic shyness: "I wonder whether the good old watchword which we heard in my youth, the old watchword of 'service,' has become quite obsolete. Has the thought of service quite lost its power to animate the minds of our young people?"

"No, I think not," replied a college dean. "In our graduating class, for example, there is

a fine group of young men who are preparing
to enter Y. M. C. A. work in Poland, and there
is another group who are going as medical missionaries to China. These men," he declared,
"are still animated by a desire to serve humanity."

No sensible person can have the slightest wish
to disparage the work of the Y. M. C. A. in
Poland or of the medical missionaries in China.
Yet one is constrained to say that the remarks of
this good dean illustrate exactly the attitude
of mind which has tended to bring the "old
watchword of service" into disrepute. I mean
this: that among the young generation there is
a growing resentment, and I think on the whole
a legitimate resentment, at the traditional
identification of service with certain definitely
limited activities of an obviously humanitarian
character, performed for the physically or
morally needy classes in foreign lands or in the
slums of great cities or backward rural districts.
These moral and medical missionaries are engaged, we all admit, in a great work, which demands devotion and self-sacrifice. But their
champions make a mistake in tactics, they dam-
age their own position, when they attempt to
set apart these special types of activitiy under a
peculiar glory of "service."

All good work, at home or abroad, in public or in private, of the hand or of the brain—all work that is done as it should be done—demands devotion and self-sacrifice and partakes of the nature of service. That so much of it is now done so feebly, so shabbily, so perfunctorily, is due to the fact that the inspiriting idea of service has never been extended to it.

What we want at present more than a fresh call to service is a wider conception of the field. Humanity has needed to have its moral and physical wounds looked after and has required ministrants to those needs since man appeared on the planet; and will always require them, and will always praise and reward, more or less, workers who supply those needs. But if humanity's adventure on the earth is ever to issue in anything more satisfying than mere self-preservation, humanity needs a multitude of other things. It needs, not least, satisfactions for a multitude of men and women who are not merely suffering bodies clamorous with physical wants but are also emotional, intellectual, and moral beings craving a higher and larger life for their special human faculties.

If the word and thought of service are to be rehabilitated, we must have new criterions of service. We cannot set apart the word for those who give food to the body and withhold it from those who give food to the mind. We cannot reserve it for those who help the sick and deny it to those who help the well. Service does not cease to be service when the intelligent and the strong are assisted. We cannot consecrate the word for ministers and teachers merely because they work for a smaller wage than presidents of railroads and singers in grand opera. Service does not cease to be service when it is remunerated. On the contrary, the world, as it grows wiser, will steadily insist on rewarding more amply all those who know how to provide what it wants. Deep in the heart of the world is a passion for discovering a larger and better life for all the people in the world, not even excluding the intellectual and other privileged classes; and every one who assists in any way at that discovery does honorable service. Furthermore, whoever bends his full strength to increasing the healthy and pleasurable life of men, sooner or later will find in his work, whatever it is, something of the peace and satisfaction of religious devotion.

In the days of one's youth, however, in one's period of apprenticeship, it is of far more importance to make oneself an effective instrument than it is to know precisely how and where the

instrument is going to be employed. Temper
the iron; sharpen the blade; and rest assured
that the world will use you by and by. Good
workmen eager for a part in the building of
civilization will not worry much about where
they are to be sent; they will desire only to be
sent where they can be used most effectively.
And they will not, for example, foolishly set
off the "service" of a good missionary against
the usefulness of a good dressmaker. A really
skilful dressmaker, I fancy, could wipe away
as many tears from human eyes as any sister
of charity.

The opposite of a life of service is not any
form of happy activity, but a slack, idle, joy-
less, half-hearted, shrinking life. There are
numerous so-called good-people who go about
to do good in such a crabbed, peevish, and melancholy fashion that contact with them makes
the day bitter and burdensome. There are, on
the other hand, persons gay and nonchalant,
who never seem to give a thought to the "still
sad music of humanity"; and yet one feels in
their presence something better than a sermon,
better than medicine, better than alms—one
feels a current of energy and joy, one feels new
power and incentive within oneself. Such persons confer a favor on mankind merely by

being alive. They add directly to the sum of
human happiness. They add to the goodness
of life. Theirs is perhaps the rarest and most
precious form of service, the most beautiful of
vocations.

Next to those who hearten us by their natural
gusto and their capacity for communicating
whatever of sweetness they find in the taste of
their own days, I would place in one class all
those who do anything whatever excellently
well. In formal ethical treatises we arrange the
members of this class in a severe hierarchy with
high places reserved for those who have held
positions of political responsibility or who have
attained eminence in science and the arts. But
we are not very realistic in our ethical treatises.
Outside the book, we find a different system of
rating. In the frank unconventional judgment
of the street, and in the tribunal of our own
hearts we find a curious equality of gratitude
and admiration for the best preacher and the
best prize fighter, the chess champion and the
prime minister, the successor of Newton and
the world's supreme tenor, the man who has
written the outstanding novel of the year, and
the baker who makes the best Parker House
rolls in town. Perhaps we even go so far as to
number among the ninety-nine worthies of the

world an extraordinary rogue or two. Certainly few of us ever purge ourselves of a lingering fondness for such eminent villains as Richard III, Cellini, Henry VIII, Ivan the Terrible, Frederick the Great, and Napoleon.

It is not of course their criminality that we admire. Paradoxical as it sounds, we seldom show ourselves such disinterested lovers of virtue as when we feel a thrill of approbation in the presence of the great criminals. We have no weak bias of a merely personal and self-interested attachment in their favour. What we respond to in them is the pure quality of their cutting intelligence, the rare hardness of their courage, the sheer potency of their will—virtues by us for once subconsciously abstracted from their practical consequences and so valued. Whenever you find yourself saying, "I like that man—I don't know why; he has almost every trait that I dislike," you may be reasonably sure that the man has also some powerful virtue which you have overlooked, or which has as yet not been listed by the professors of ethics. For the popular and undiscriminating idolization of athletes, dancers, singers, marksmen, poets, jockeys, and supreme bakers there is this justification: each one of these heroes has demonstrated for the time the utmost capacity of the

human body or mind in that direction. He has
established a standard. He has set us a mark
which enables us to look with equanimity upon
any one who does not approach it or surpass it.
To throw fifty successive "ringers" at quoits is
a feat requiring an almost godlike faculty.
There are few services higher than demonstrat-
ing the utmost capacities of the human spirit;
and it is a sound popular instinct which ap-
plauds such demonstrations, even in matters
which impress the censorious as trivial.

"But suppose," objects a wary moralist, "suppose a man wishes to demonstrate the utmost
capacity of the human spirit for being a tiger or
a snake. Should you applaud that experiment?" No, I should not applaud that experiment. I should do *mon possible* to dissuade the
aspirant from that, and I should proceed in this
way. I should first lead him through a zoö-
logical garden to the cage of the Bengal tiger
and the python; and I should say: "Here is a
far better tiger, and here is a far better snake
than you can ever hope to become by the utmost
stretch of your tigerish or reptilian pro-
pensities. You will make no inspiring con-
tribution by this experiment. You will bungle
towards it and fail short. An unsurpassable
mark has already been set by the framer of this

"dreadful symmetry." But why not go in for aeronautics? It does look as if we might eventually surpass the eagle in flight. And the desire to get above the earth has always impressed me as a very human, though a dangerous, passion. If, however, danger and difficulty really attract you, why not go in for the big experiment? It is much more difficult than becoming a python or a tiger. Why not attempt to demonstrate the utmost capacity of the human spirit for being a man?"

But let us descend from the dizzy heights where the heroes and villains dwell. Few of us can belong to that eminent class which sets new standards of human achievement. Below that high level, however, is the wide workaday world where professional competence is ever in request and ample scope is afforded for the display of a relative excellence. Educators of the Renaissance ordinarily composed their outlines of education with a prince in their mind's eye, who was to be instructed in every art and science necessary or becoming to a member of the governing class. In a democratic society, as every one knows, the assumption is that we are all peers, that we are all princes, that each one of us is to be trusted with some share of the burden of the political and social government. Under the influence of that assumption, we take an ever broader view of the useful activities of men. As our humanism becomes democratic, our snobism dwindles, the number of "base" activities declines, we begin to recognize all those workmen as engaged in "gentle" or "noble" enterprise who are spending themselves for the stability and growth of the commonwealth. The circumstance makes it steadily easier for each man to choose a vocation according to his nature, and so to discharge at the same time his duty to the State and his responsibility to his own individual "genius."

Failure to recognize how near at hand and how rich and various the fields of service are is responsible for much of the unhappiness and unrest which many young people feel between the ages of twenty and twenty-five. It is customary for old people to add to the confusion of the young by talking to them about the happiness of youth. They say, amiable but sentimental grey-beards say, to a youth of twenty: "Enjoy yourself now while you can. You are now in the happiest years of your life." If I were addressing an audience on the verge of twenty, I should say: Distrust these sentimental old people. Don't believe a word of all this. In all probability your most happy and fruitful days are still to come. If you gird yourselves now strictly and austerely for the tasks of spring-time, it is more than likely that after the age of twenty-five you will find the years growing, for all their shocks and accidents, steadily richer and sweeter in their main substance, to the end. I think it hardly doubtful that most of you are now, in the early twenties, in your most restless and unhappy period. Why? Well, for a most interesting reason: because, as Emerson says, "All young persons thirst for a real existence for an object—for something great and good which they shall do with their heart."

You are at precisely the period when one casts about most earnestly for something great and good to do with one's heart. You have considered many possibilities, yet you hang in the doldrums of indecision. As yet, you have not found any object within your reach which seems great and good enough to command a life's devotion. You sigh for definite objects which you know are not for you, or you seethe with vague desires for dim unattainable things. You are unhappy because you still stand with arms wide-outstretched to embrace the infinite. You have not yet soberly reflected upon the elementary physical and spiritual truth that it is only by closing your arms and resolutely shutting most of the infinite out that you can really embrace and keep anything. You have not yet taken to heart the great maxim of Goethe: "It is within limits that the master first shows his mastership." You are still fighting against that law of nature which fixes the pain of choice as the cost of every practical step forward.

Meanwhile you hear from men of a certain narrow intensity a disquieting summons to a self-sacrificing life of service, a summons to precisely that form of service in which these "dreadful summoners" have themselves attained the fullest self-realization. While you are under the spell of their exhortation, the definite things at hand which you can now do well, or which you are now learning to do well, seem small and humdrum and mean. And some of you, perhaps, with a real talent for millinery or landscape gardening are considering whether you ought not to renounce these talents and go to China as medical missionaries. And some of you with a talent for chemical investigation or stockbreeding are wondering whether you ought not to renounce these talents, and, chanting the old song, "Nothing in my hands I bring," devote yourselves to spreading the gospel among the Buddhists.* A great many more of you, I suppose, have a beautiful genius for an occupation more various than that of Leonardo da Vinci and the many-sided men of the Renaissance. I mean the occupation of domestic managership, including in one endlessly versatile person the professions of wife, mother, nurse, dietitian, milliner, tailor, economist, artist, architect, teacher, religious guide, counsellor, and dictator—I have mentioned only a few of the activities which every competent matriarch undertakes. Yet many of you, I suspect, with a real talent for this rich life of high and varied service, in which every virtue and every charm count, many of you have been persuaded that this life is not service but servitude, and are considering whether you should not renounce your beautiful talent and devote yourselves to selling bonds or writing for the short-story magazines. "I don't want to spend all my life washing dishes," you have cried—as if washing dishes were a hundredth part of the fascinating things you are expected to do!

I suspect this unrest to be present among the

---

*I recently received an illumination when one of my Japanese friends remarked casually of a fellow student from Nippon that after a preliminary survey of Christianity and Buddhism, he had embraced Christianity because: "It is so much easier—to be a Buddhist you have to study."

younger generation because I hear of it constantly. Recently one of the most interesting and intelligent members of a graduating class came to me to talk, as she said, about her future. "I have spent," she said, "four years at the University. Now they want me to go home and marry and settle down and be 'just a good woman.' My home-town will sweep over me and swallow up everything that I have learned in my years here. *I don't want to be a good woman!*" "What *do* you want to be ?" I enquired. She could not phrase the answer promptly. But she had both arms extended towards the infinite. And by that token I could tell well enough that what she wanted was "something great and good that she should do with her heart."

Now, every educator who is worth his salt knows that this hungry discontent of one-and-twenty indicates in the hopefullest way that education is "taking." But it indicates also that education is still incomplete. It indicates that imagination has not yet surveyed realistically the field of service. A girl of twenty who stands with arms wide-stretched towards the infinite is usually thinking secretly of New York or Chicago, which are by no means infinite. And so the small towns and provincial

cities are stripped of the bright, tempered instruments necessary for their regeneration; and
the great metropolis is crowded too full for
elbow-room. I think the next step in our higher
education must be the effective preaching of a
"new provincialism." I think we need to show
our graduates the field for service and the large
opportunity for the increase of happiness by
carrying their college and university training
back to the home-town, and making the new
standards prevail there. The mentally poor and
needy should perhaps go to the metropolis and
receive. But the essentially rich may safely remain in the provinces and give. The greater
your talent, the better you can afford to strike
root where you are.

Our democratic theory is that American life
should taste good at all points in the States.
We cannot tolerate the idea of a rich and intellectual capital of highly civilized people sur-
rounded by an immense population of peasants
and yokels. Already many conveniences of our
material civilization have penetrated the remote countryside. Already one can buy as good
gasoline, soap, shredded wheat biscuit, and tobacco in Gopher Prairie and Sleepy Eye as in
New York City. But we want more than that.
We want to be able to get as good talk, as good

books and magazines, as good music, as good
health, exercise, and recreation, as respectable
schools, and as cheerful homes with lawns and
abundance of flowers and trees in Gopher
Prairie and in Sleepy Eye as in New York City
or Stockbridge. This object is perfectly attain-
able. It will be attained just as soon as the
beautiful vague imaginations of our hungry
young people become positive, realistic, and
practical; just as soon as they clasp their wide-
stretched arms and hold fast the good that is
within reach.

Two girls of my acquaintance who can write
a little are now looking towards going to New
York as the great adventure. "If all goes well,"
they will soon be living in a six-by-eight bed-
room on 120th Street, and they will be writing
fourth-rate stories for fourth-rate magazines;
and the great metropolis will sweep over them
and leave not a trace to mark the place where
they sink.

The trouble with these young women is not
that they have "aspirations," but that they are
insufficiently and unrealistically ambitious. For
the sake of expressing their mediocrity, they
are abandoning a chance to express their excellence. After a good course in domestic science,
these same girls, let us say, might go into some

squalid, fly-infested, half-civilized town of the great Border; set up a clean, modern, scientific, attractive tea-room and cafeteria; and gradually teach the entire town what to eat, how to cook, how to serve meals, and how to behave at table. Or, let us say for the sake of those who savor their "idealism" more in the abstract than in the concrete: three hundred and sixty-five days in the year, they might bring something of grace, cleanliness, charm, and civility into the lives of an entire community. They might contribute permanently and substantially to the advance of civilization.

And they might actually have turned to this enterprise with imaginative gusto and practical effectiveness if work of this sort had ever been related in their minds to their "suppressed desire" for that enchanting will-o'-the-wisp, a beautiful and heroic life. The "service" as I state it here does not kindle the imagination like the thought of Florence Nightingale organizing her hospital in the Crimean War, nor like the thought of Jenny Lind contributing the glory of her voice to charity; but if there is one sound principle of human economy, it is this: To save a man from death or even to make him ecstatically happy once or twice, is a small service compared with making him comfortable and contented and civilized every day of his life.

For some years I had in my house a bright young Japanese student who was preparing to be an engineer. He was not a Christian, but he had a tincture of Buddhism, and he used to come in from time to time and ask for some book "about culture." He received his degree with honors, and began his apprenticeship in one of our great electrical manufacturing establishments. From there he wrote me a remarkably interesting letter, interesting for two reasons: first, because it illustrates the deep-seated human passion to be of use; and, second, it illustrates the common human inability to recognize the usefulness of the tools within one's hand. Here is a portion of the letter:

I want to ask you the following, on which you may smile again. It is the similar question to that which I once did while I stayed yours: What is the Life? and how we have to live up in this world? Once I told you that I have to live for the sake of others, at least within my own scope. Although I think it ought to be, the idea is very vague and I am still doubting how I can go at it, in spite of the fact that I am so poor both materially and intellectually, as I have hardly help my own self. This is mainly, I think, due to the lack of any strong belief in any of the religions. Thus things do not seem very real but as virtual vision. I have inter-

ested in religion, philosophy, and literature,
but I cannot comprehend why I do not get into
enthusiastic enough to obtain from either religious belief or philosophical reason the sound
composure of my own mind. . . . Engineer
as I am, cannot entirely be managed away from
the material environment: there is always certain contradiction between the ideal and material views, which means the fighting or uneasi-
ness in the soul."

I said to this Japanese boy, so anxious to live
for others yet so poor that he could hardly help
himself, and so torn by the "fighting in his own
soul" that he was losing even the capacity for
self-help: "The remedy is very simple. You
wish to serve the world. Well, you know one
way to serve it. Japan needs electric lights.
You know how to make them. Throw the full
strength of your soul and body into making good
electric lights, and you will have performed
your best service to the world. In this material
environment in which we all must work, there is
no more shining avenue of 'service' open to you
than to become a good engineer and to work
manfully at that." Advice of this sort, I know
well enough, will bring no immediate comfort
to the romantic mind which yearns for "the land
where I am not," and which has established no
working terms with the material environment;

but it may lead in the long run to a fruitful reconsideration of the relation between usefulness and the special powers of the individual. And it is advice which may be given, *mutatis mutandis,* with just as much pertinence to a poet as to an engineer.

It is a platitude, which nevertheless each generation has to discover afresh, that one serves the world best by doing eagerly what one can do best, and not something else. Therefore Pindar gave as a rule of life this injunction: "Become what you are." It is not quite so simple as it sounds, to become what one is. Most of us are creatures moving about in worlds half-realized—only half-conscious, only half-emerged from our own dullness and indolence and inefficiency. We do not know what we want or what we can do because we do not know clearly what we are. Meanwhile we play the ape and the parrot to our companions. We become creatures of convention and careless habit. We accept the task work thrusts into our empty hands by whatever busy man passes our way. We become what our parents were or what our neighbors are. We make a virtue of our indolence, and call a lazy yielding to chance or a passive drifting with the stream, a patient acceptance of destiny. This destiny is a weak-hearted old-fashioned god whom educated men and women are sent into the world to dethrone. This destiny dwells in the past or lurks furtively in the environment, and is not ours. The only destiny which a man of grit will allow to influence him much is his destination. Our chance of reaching our destination does not lie in the line of what is ordinarily called renunciation and martyrdom, but rather in the discovery of our own inmost desires and our true powers and in the resolute organization of our lives around them. It ought to be a platitude that this is also the way to make ourselves the most useful instruments for the world's work.

The wary moralist, whom I have quoted before, here interjects a remonstrance against my dismissal of all those priceless virtues involved in "renunciation and martyrdom." I am glad that he does; for he gives me occasion to declare that I do not dismiss these virtues. On the contrary I propose to put them to the hardest possible use. Instead of advocating renunciation and martyrdom for the purpose of becoming a nonentity, I am advocating renunciation and, if need be, martyrdom for the purpose of becoming an entity. There is no course which demands more resolute power of abnegation than the course which leads to becoming what you

VOCATION 193

are. In order to become an individual, you must cease to be a crowd. You must learn the law of self-integration and loyally obey it. You must hurry past all the flowery by-paths into which the conflicting crowd of your own instincts tries to tempt you. At every fork in the road, you will find some one crying, "Come this way!" At every oasis in desert lands, you will hear a beguiling invitation to tarry there or wait awhile. And nothing will get you by— not eyes blindfolded nor ears stopped with wax —nothing but an imperative sense of "mission," nothing but a lively sense of the appointed service which you are to perform by reaching your destination.

Scrutinize yourself mercilessly and find out what you really are before you commit yourself. Don't lie to yourself about that. But when you have found out, insist upon it. "He that rides his hobby gently," as Emerson says, "must always give way to him that rides his hobby hard." If you are really a missionary to the Chinese, put your life on the cast of that die. China does not wish to be served by cowards. If you are really by nature and instinct and talent a toe-dancer, be a toe-dancer with all your might. If you are really that, you will probably put more of a "kick" into toe-dancing than into anything else. Chesterfield's exhortation to his son to "shine" somewhere may be taken to heart even by a bootblack. If you are sure that you are called to be a teacher, put your entire capital into that investment. If you are a poet, by all means become one, body and soul. If you are really "domestic," put your heart into domesticity; and don't expect praise for doing even a multitude of little things ill. So far as my observation goes, young people with a modern liberal education can usually do several things fairly well. If you are in doubt which thing you do best, it is wiser to resort to an oracle than to hang in perpetual uncertainty or to flutter in eternal oscillation. Draw lots for the best of two guesses, and then abide by the lot.

Lay out the line of your own destiny. Then work faithfully on that line year after year with the zeal for improvement and the love of excellence which open the doors of a natural aristocracy; and you may rest assured that twenty years hence in your own circle, in your own community, you will be one of the "indispensable" members of your generation. When you have patiently perfected your own usefulness, you need not fear that you will not be used. Your special instrument of service and all your virtues and all your charms will be called for

and taken at one time or another, in one place
or another, for the purposes of the better human
society which we are eager to create. In the
period of your apprenticeship, it behooves you
to meditate upon the means of self-perfection,
upon becoming what you are, rather than upon
rewards or glory or even upon service. But if
when you present yourselves at the door of the
next age, you offer to concentrate all that you
have and are upon the task which you can do
best, you will not have to wait for good fortune.
You yourselves are good fortune.

VIII

THE POINT OF VIEW IN AMERICAN CRITICISM

Were you looking to be held together by lawyers?
Or by argument on paper? or by arms?
Nay, nor the world, nor any living thing, will so cohere.
                                                WHITMAN.

The teacher of the coming age must occupy himself in the study and explanation of the moral constitution of man more than in the elucidation of difficult texts.

                                                EMERSON.

There is that in me—I do not know what it is—but I know it is
    in me.
Wrench'd and sweaty—calm and cool then my body becomes;
I sleep—I sleep long.
I do not know it—it is without a name—it is a word unusual;
It is not in any dictionary, utterance, symbol.
Something it swings on more than the earth I swing on;
To it the creation is the friend whose embracing awakes me.
Perhaps I might tell more. Outlines! I plead for my brothers
    and sisters.
Do you see, O my brothers and sisters?
It is not chaos or death—it is form, union, plan—it is eternal life
    —it is Happiness.

                                                WHITMAN.

THE POINT OF VIEW IN AMERICAN CRITICISM*

According to all the critics, domestic and foreign, who have prophesied against America during the last hundred years, the great and ever-present danger of a democratic society lies in its tendency to destroy high standards of excellence and to accept the average man as a satisfactory measure of all things. Instead of saying, like Antigone in the drama of Sophocles, 'I know I please the souls I ought to please,' democracy, we are told, is prone to dismiss the question whether she has any high religious obligation, and to murmur complacently, 'I know I please the souls of average men.' I propose to examine a little the origins of this belief, and then to inquire whether it is justified by the present condition of our civilization, as reflected in our current literature. In the course of the inquiry I shall at least raise the question whether the average man is as easy to please as he is ordinarily supposed to be.

* Delivered as a lecture on the William Vaughn Moody foundation at the University of Chicago, May 10, 1922.

At the very foundation of the Republic, the menace of the average man was felt by a distinguished group of our own superior men, including Washington, John Adams, Hamilton, and many other able and prosperous country gentlemen. To them the voice of the people was not the voice of God, but the clamor of a hydra-headed monster, requiring to be checked and bridled. Thus, at the outset of our civilization, they established a point of view and they instituted a criticism, which were unfriendly to the average man and his aspirations and to all his misguided friends. They possessed, for example, certain standards of character and manners, which they applied with some austerity to what they regarded as the vulgar Jacobinism of Thomas Paine, to the disintegrating demagoguery of Jefferson, to the cosmopolitan laxity of Franklin, and to all the tendencies of French radicalism towards leveling by law the inequalities created by law and by nature.

Edmund Burke explained England's relative immunity to the equalitarian speculations of the French by this fact: 'We continue,' he said, 'as in the last two ages, to read more generally, than, I believe, is now done on the Continent, the authors of sound antiquity. These occupy our minds. They give us another taste and turn,

and will not suffer us to be more than transiently
amused with paradoxical morality.' Now, it is
insufficiently recognized that, in the third quarter of the eighteenth century, America, like
England, was at the height of her classical period—I mean the period when statesmen, poets,
and painters most deliberately and successfully
imitated the example of the ancients. The public characters of Washington and his friends,
like those of Burke and his friends, were in
the grand style, were in a style more or less
consciously moulded upon that of the great republicans of England, Rome, and Athens.
From Cromwell and Milton, and, above all,
from the heroes of Plutarch, the friends of
Washington inherited the ardor and the elevation of their public spirit, and, at the same
time, their lofty disdain for the vulgar herd and
a conviction that the salvation of the people de-
pended upon the perpetuation of their own
superiorities.

At its best, near the source, and on its positive
side, there is something very august and inspiring in the utterances of this old Roman or
aristocratic republicanism. It is not far from
its best in the letters of Abigail Adams.

Glory, my son [she writes to John Quincy
Adams], in a country which has given birth to

characters, both in the civil and military departments, which may vie with the wisdom and valor of antiquity. As an immediate descendant of one of these characters, may you be led to an imitation of that disinterested patriotism and that noble love of country, which will teach you to despise wealth, titles, pomp, and equipage, as mere external advantages, which cannot add to the excellence of your mind, or compensate for the want of integrity or virtue.

It is not difficult to despise 'wealth, pomp, and equipage,' when one is adequately supplied with them; John Quincy Adams, accordingly, found his occasion for pride in the excellence of his mind and in his integrity and virtue. And, true to his breeding, he maintained, like Coriolanus, a kind of passionate and scornful opposition to the vulgar mob. In 1795, he writes to his mother that France will remain without the means to form a Constitution till she has exploded the doctrine of submission to and veneration for public opinion. A little later, he admits to his father that 'the struggle against a popular clamor is not without its charms in my mind.'

There he sounds the rallying cry of our great conservative tradition. I shall not ask here whether the creative ardor of the aristocratic spirit which we observed in the mother is not already beginning to be transformed in the son to a certain ardor of repression. Nor am I concerned here to trace the evolution of this Roman-American pride from its pure high source, down through the ages, till it reappears in aristocratic republicans of our own times, who still find a charm in opposing the popular clamor. I am thinking of the railway magnate, author of the celebrated phrase, 'The public be damned'; and I am thinking of our most aggressive literary critic, a professed Federalist, who remarked the other day in language savoring a bit, perhaps, of the Roman decadence: 'I don't care a damn what happens to the Republic after I am dead.'

We must pause here, however, long enough to recall that the classical models of society, which the more conservative of our forefathers kept in their minds' eye, rested upon a slave population, and that the government which they actually set up countenanced, in opposition to the plebeian taste of Paine and the demagoguery of Jefferson, a slave population. It is a question of more than academic interest to-day, whether or not the government which they set up necessarily implies the continued existence of an illiterate peasantry.

Those who believe that the salvation of the

people depends upon the perpetuation of their own superiorities are likely, in the long run, to make the end subservient to the means, to grow rather careless about the salvation of the people and rather over-careful about the preservation of their own superiorities. They incline, also, to a belief that these superiorities can best be perpetuated through their own offspring—a belief which, so far as I can learn, is inadequately supported by statistics. On this assumption, however, they endeavor to make a kind of closed corporation of their own class, and seek to monopolize for it the administration of government, the possession of property, the enjoyment of higher education and culture, and the literary production of the country.

These tendencies, as we know, appeared very early in the history of the Republic. John Adams nearly ruined himself in 1787 by his frank declaration that wealth and birth should be qualifications for the Senate. Hamilton, at the same time, put forth his proposals for restraining the vulgar herd by perpetuating wealth and the leadership of established families in the nearest possible American imitation of the British monarchical and aristocratic system.

The irrepressible conflict provoked by such

attempts to check the rich fecundity and the unpredictable powers of our colonial 'populace' is ordinarily presented to us as a contention over political principles. In its most comprehensive aspect, it may profitably be regarded as rather a conflict of religions. The short interval between the adoption of the Constitution and the end of the eighteenth century is the period of antique Republicanism triumphant, dominated by the religion of the superior man. In 1800, this religion received a blow in the election of Jefferson, the St. Paul of the religion of the populace, who preached faith, hope, and charity for the masses. In 1828, the religion of the superior man received a still more ominous blow, when the fiery, pistoling rough-rider from Tennessee, Andrew Jackson, defeated John Quincy Adams. At this reverse to the sons of light, John Quincy Adams lost his faith in God, the God of superior men.

We have recently had, from the fourth eminent generation of the Adams family, Brooks, Charles Francis, and Henry, a voluminous commentary upon the effort of 'the heirs of Washington' to stand against the popular clamor and uphold their great tradition. On the whole, if we may trust their testimony, it has been a tragically unavailing effort. In Boston and

Cambridge and in a few tributary villages, in old New York and Washington, on a few great plantations of Virginia and the Carolinas, the civilization which the superior men contemplated obtained a struggling foothold before the Civil War. And this civilization achieved some literary expression in the classical oratory of Webster, in the fine old English gentility of Irving's prose, and in the pale provincial flowering of our New England poetry. Sanguine observers saw in this literary renascence promise that the intrenched intelligence and culture of the settled, civilized East was to take and hold the mastery in the national life.

But for Henry Adams, at least, that hope ended with his return from England in 1868. He discovered, when he went to Washington to offer his services in carrying on the great tradition—he discovered that the great tradition was broken. There had taken place, not merely a Civil War, but a far more fundamental revolution. He and his kind, bred on the classics, and versed in law and European diplomacy, were anachronisms, survivors out of the classical eighteenth century, belated revelers in the Capitol. A multitude of unknown or ignored forces had developed in his absence, and had combined to antiquate him, to extrude him from the cur-

rent of national life, and to incapacitate him
for a place in the public councils. This singular
new nation was no respecter of grandfathers.
It took its superior men wherever it found them.
It picked its chief statesman out of a log cabin
in Illinois, its chief military hero out of an
Ohio tannery, its most eminent poet from a car-
penter's shop, and its leading man of letters
from a pilot-house on the Mississippi. Such
standards! Henry spent a life-time elaborating
his grand principle of the degradation of energy,
to explain to himself why the three grandsons of
two presidents of the United States all ended
miserably: one as President of the Kansas City
Stock Yards; one as a member of the Massa-
chusetts Bar; while one had sunk to the level of
a Professor of History at Harvard.

From the point of view of these antique republicans, the period from the Civil War to
the end of the nineteenth century proves the
truth of all the prophesies against the average
man. This is the period of triumphant democracy—meaning, of course, the triumph, not
of the political party, but of the religious principle. In this epoch, the gates of opportunity
open as never before to the populace, to the new
men. What are the results? Throughout the
period, the steadily waning influence of Eastern

intelligence and culture in the national life, steadily increasing immigration from the peasant stocks of Europe, expansion of the population into new western territory, prosperity of industrial pioneers, rise of the railway magnate, the iron-master, the organizer of large-scale production of material commodities—immense rewards and glory for supplying the average man what the average man, at that particular moment, wanted and had to have

Midway in this epoch, one of its heroes, Andrew Carnegie, wrote a book which he called *Triumphant Democracy*—a work which exults and rejoices in the goodness and greatness of American life. It was an industrial captain's reply to the foreign critics who had flitted across the country year after year, like ravens, boding disaster. It was a reply from the point of view of a Scotch radical, a self-made man, who could compare the poor little Scotch town of Dunfermline, where the revolution in machinery had ruined his father, to the booming city of Pittsburgh, Pennsylvania, where the same revolution had made him one of the masters of his generation.

Carnegie's point of view was inadequate. He offered no effective answer to the savage criticism which Dickens had made of our civilization forty years earlier, when he pictured the democracy as brutal, boisterous, boastful, ignorant, and hypocritical. He made no effective reply to Carlyle, who had cried twenty-two years later than Dickens, 'My friend, brag not yet of our American cousins! Their quantity of cotton, dollars, industry and resources, I believe to be almost unspeakable; but I can by no means worship the like of these.'   . ,

Matthew Arnold, a critical friend of ours, far more friendly to our political institutions and to our social organization than Carlyle, dropped in upon us at about the time that Carnegie published his book. 'The trouble with Carnegie and his friends,' said Arnold, 'is that they have no conception of the chief defect of American life; namely, that it is so dreadfully uninteresting.' This dullness, he explained, was due to the average man's quite inadequate conception of the good life, which did not go beyond being diligent in business and serving the Lord—making money and observing a narrow code of morality.

The particularly hopeless aspect of our case, Arnold thought, was that we, as a people, seemed quite unconscious of our deficiencies on the human side of our civilization. We displayed a self-satisfaction which is 'vulgarizing and retarding.' Nationally we were boasters, or, as we say nowadays, 'boosters.' 'The worst of it is,' he continues, 'that this tall talk and self-glorification meets with hardly any rebuke from sane criticism over there.' He cites some examples; and then he adds that, 'the new West promises to beat in the game of brag even the stout champions I have been quoting.'

Now, no Englishman will ever fathom the mystery of Uncle Sam's boasting. No outsider can ever know, as we all know, how often, out of the depths of self-distrust and self-contempt and cutting self-criticism, he has whistled to keep his courage up in the dark, and has smiled reassuringly while his heart was breaking. Still, if you look into the literature of the period, you find that there is much warrant for Arnold's strictures, though not always precisely where he found it. The little boasts of men like Lowell and Thomas Wentworth Higginson and Brander Matthews are only Yankee whistling, the turning of the trodden worm, a decent pride in the presence of 'a certain condescension in foreigners.' Lowell knew a man, he says, who thought Cambridge the best spot on the habitable globe. 'Doubtless God could have made a better, but doubtless He never did.' I myself am fond of declaring that the campus of the

University of Illinois is finer than the meadows of Christ Church College, Oxford. But no one in America thinks anything a whit the finer for what an academic person has said in its favor. Nor, on the other hand, does anyone, outside academic circles, think anything in America a whit the worse for what a foreign critic has said against it. The Chicago journalists, for example, with true Jacksonian hilarity, ridiculed Arnold and, after his departure, stigmatized him as a 'cur.'

The only criticism which ever, as we say, 'gets across' to the Jacksonian democracy is that which comes from one of their own number. The really significant aspects of our self-complacency in Carnegie's time were reflected in the popular literature of the period by writers sprung from the new democracy, self-made authors, who flattered the average man into satisfaction with his present state and his average achievement. I am thinking of Western writers, like Joaquin Miller and Riley and Carleton and Bret Harte and Mark Twain. I am thinking of the romantic glamour which these men contrived to spread over the hard rough life and the rougher characters of the middle-borderers, the Argonauts, and the Forty-Niners.

You recall the method. First, they admit certain facts—for picturesque effect. For example, these settlers of the Golden West, they say, included a few decent men, but they were in great part the riffraff of the world—foreign adventurers, offscourings of Eastern cities, uncouth, red-shirted illiterates from the Middle States, lawless, dirty, tobacco-spitting, blaspheming, drunken, horse-thieves, murderers, and gamblers. And then, with noble poetic vision, they cry: 'But what delicacy of sentiment beneath those shaggy bosoms! What generosity and chivalry under those old red shirts! Horse-thieves, yet nature's noblemen! Gamblers and drunkards, yet kings of men!' 'I say to you,' chants 'the poet of the Sierras,' 'that there is nothing in the pages of history so glorious, so entirely grand, as the lives of these noble Spartan fathers and mothers of Americans, who begot and brought forth and bred the splendid giants of the generation that is now fast following the setting sun of their unselfish and all immortal lives.'

Here is the point of view of the Jacksonian democracy in its romantic mood. This, in general, was the point of view of Mark Twain, the most original force in American letters and, on the whole, the most broadly representative

American writer between the close of the Civil War and the end of the century. Most of us have enough pioneer blood in our veins, or in our imaginative sympathies, to love Mark Twain nowadays. But academic people, they tell us,—and they tell us truly,—had little to do with establishing his earlier reputation. He neither flattered them nor pleased them. He pleased and flattered and liberated the emotions of that vast mass of the population which had been suppressed and inarticulate. He was the greatest booster for the average man that the country ever produced. Confident in the political and mechanical and natural superiorities conferred upon every son of these States by his mere birth under the American flag, Mark Twain laughed at the morality of France, the language of Germany, the old masters of Italy, the caste system of India, the imperialism of England, the romances of Scott, the penal laws of the sixteenth century, and at the chivalry of the court of King Arthur—he laughed at all the non-American world, from the point of view of the average American, stopping only from time to time to pat his countrymen on the back and to cry, like Jack Horner, 'What a brave boy am I!' To make a climax to the bold irreverence of this Jacksonian laughter, he laughed at New England and at all her starchy immortals.

In the *Connecticut Yankee at King Arthur's Court,* published in 1889, we hear the last full-hearted laughter of triumphant democracy. Twain himself became sombre in his later years; he became cynical, and touched with misanthropy. I cannot go here, in any detail, into the causes for the darkening of his outlook. The most interesting of these causes, perhaps, was that Mark Twain had one foot over the threshold of a new age, our present era, which I shall call the era of critical and pessimistic democracy.   He had begun to emerge, as I think we are all now beginning to emerge, from the great romantic illusion about the average man, namely, that liberty or equality or any kind of political recognition or literary exploitation, or even economic independence, can make him a happy or a glorious being.

Poets and novelists, since the French Revolution, have fostered this romantic illusion in a laudable but misdirected effort to bestow dignity upon the humblest units of humanity. They liberated the emotion for a religion of democracy. They did little to give to that emotion intelligent direction.

You will recall Wordsworth's poem called

'Resolution and Independence.' The poet, wandering on the moor in richly gloomy thought, comes upon a poor old man, bent, broken, leaning over a pool, gathering leeches for his livelihood. The poet questions him how it goes with him. The old man replies, quietly enough, that it goes pretty hard, that it is going rather worse; but that he still perseveres and manages to get on, in one way or another. Whereupon Wordsworth falls into a kind of visionary trance. The old peasant looms for him to a gigantic stature. He becomes the heroic 'man with the hoe'; a shadowy shape against the sky; man in the abstract, clothed in all the moral splendor of the poet's own imagination.

This same trick of the fancy Hardy plays with his famous dairy-maid, Tess of the D'Urbervilles. She is but an ignorant, instinctive, erring piece of Eve's flesh. Yet, says Hardy, drawing upon the riches of his own poetic associations, 'The impressionable peasant leads a larger, fuller, more dramatic life than the pachydermatous king.' Thereupon he proceeds to invest the dairy-maid with the tragic emotions and import of a heroine of Thebes or Pelops' line. He infers, by a poetic fallacy, that she is as interesting and as significant to herself as she is to him.

I will take one other case, the hero of a recently translated novel, Knut Hamsun's *Growth of the Soil*. Here we have an illiterate peasant of Norway, going into the public land almost empty-handed; gradually acquiring a pig, a cow, a woman, a horse, building a turf-shelter, a cowshed, a cabin, a mill—and so, little by little, toiling like an ox, becoming a prosperous farmer, owner of rich lands and plentiful flocks and herds. It is, in a sense, a very cheerful book, a sort of new *Robinson Crusoe*. Its moral appears to be that, so long as men stick to the soil and preserve their ignorance and their natural gusto, they may be happy. It is a glorification of the beaver, the building animal. It is an idealization of the peasant at the instinctive level.

The trick of the literary imagination in all these cases is essentially the same as that which Bret Harte played with his Argonauts, and Miller and Riley with their Indiana pioneers, and Mark Twain with his Connecticut Yankee. We are changing all that.

I chanced the other day upon an impressive new American novel, strikingly parallel in some respects to Hamsun's *Growth of the Soil,* but utterly different from it in the mood and the point of view. I refer to the story of Kansas life, called *Dust,* by Mr. and Mrs. Haldeman-Julius. Here again we have the hardy pioneer, rough, dirty, and capable, entering on the new land, with next to nothing but his expectations; acquiring a pig, a hut, cattle, and a wife; and gradually 'growing up with the country' into a prosperous western farmer, with stock in the bank, and a Cadillac, and electric lights in the cowbarns, and kerosene lamps in the house. Our human beaver in America, toiling with the same ox-like fortitude as Isak in Norway, achieves the same material success. But—and this is the difference—the story is one of unrelieved gloom ending in bitter tragedy. Why this sustained note of gloom? Why has our Kansas tale none of the happy gusto of Hamsun's *Growth of the Soil?* Because the Kansas farmer is not content with the life of a peasant. Because our Kansas authors refuse to glorify man on the instinctive level, or to disguise the essential poverty and squalor of his personal life with a poetic fallacy. The book is written from a point of view at which it is apparent that our civilization has failed to solve the human problem.

Since the time of *The Connecticut Yankee* and Carnegie's *Triumphant Democracy,* our literary interpreters have been gradually shifting their ground. They are giving us now a criticism of life from a position at which it is possible to see through the poetic illusion about the average man. Making an effort now to see him as he really is, our authors are reporting that he is not satisfied with his achievements, he is not happy, he is very miserable. The most hopeful aspect of American literature to-day is its widespread pessimism. I call this symptom hopeful, because it is most fully exhibited by precisely that part of the country, and by those elements of the population, which were thought forty years ago to be most addicted to boasting and most deeply infected with the vulgarizing and retarding self-complacency of the Philistine, the red-shirted Jacksonian from Missouri. This pessimism comes out of Wisconsin, Minnesota, Illinois, Indiana, Missouri, Kansas, and California; from the sons and daughters of pioneer farmers, country doctors, small-town lawyers, and country editors; from the second generation of immigrant stock, German, Swedish, Scotch, Irish; from the hungry, nomadic semi-civilization of the West.

I call this Western pessimism auspicious, because it is so sharply critical, and because the criticism is directed, not so much against the political and economic framework of society as

against the kind of personalities which this society produces, and against the quantity and
quality of the human satisfactions which these
personalities have at their disposal.   It is directed against that defect in our civilization
which Arnold pointed out; it is so lacking in
elevation and beauty; it is so humdrum, so
dreadfully uninteresting; it so fails to appease
the vague yet already acutely painful hunger
of the average man for a good life.   'Beguile
us no longer,' cry the new voices; 'beguile us
no longer with heroic legends and romantic
idyls. The life which you celebrate is not beautiful, not healthy, not satisfying.   It is ugly,
obscene, devastating.   It is driving us mad.
And we are going to revolt from it.'

The manifestation of this spirit which, at the
present moment, is attracting most attention is
what Mr. Van Doren, in his interesting book on
Contemporary American Novelists, has called
'the revolt from the village.' I need only remind
you of that long series of narratives, beginning
in the early eighties with E. W. Howe's *Story
of a Country Town,* and followed by Hamlin
Garland's *Main Travelled Roads,* Mr. Masters's *Spoon River Anthology,* Sherwood An-
derson's *Winesburg, Ohio,* Sinclair Lewis's
Main Street, Zona Gale's *Miss Lulu Bett,* and

the novel of which I have already spoken, *Dust,*
by Mr. and Mrs. Haldeman-Julius.

But the interesting pessimistic and critical
note in our current literature is by no means confined to representations of country life and the
small town. Take Mrs. Wharton's pictures of
metropolitan society, from *The House of Mirth*
to *The Age of Innocence,* remembering only
that Mrs. Wharton cannot be classed as a Jacksonian; then consider the dreary wide wilderness of Mr. Dreiser's picture of big business;
Ben Hecht's story of a city-editor in *Erik Dorn;*
Mr. Cabell's *Cream of the Jest;* Mr. Norris's
broad picture of the California scene in *Brass;*
Mr. Fitzgerald's account of the younger generation in *The Beautiful and Damned;* Mr.
Hergesheimer's admirable new novel, *Cytherea;*
and, finally, Mr. Lewis's *Babbitt.*

Here we are invited to consider a class of
which the discontent cannot be explained by
their struggle with the churlishness of the soil
and the rigor and tragic whimsicality of the elements. Most of the characters, indeed, have
reached a level at which even the economic
struggle is as much a pastime as a necessity.
They are business men and their womenkind,
with a sprinkling of professional men, people
who, as we say, know 'how to live,' people who

live expensively, purchasing with free hand whatever gratifications are available for the senses. Nevertheless, if we may trust their interpreters, these people, too, are dreadfully uninteresting to one another, alternating between a whipped-up excitement and a stifled yawn. Their entire stratum of society is permeated by a terrible ennui. Jaded with business and card-parties, Mr. Hergesheimer's persons, for example, can conceive no relief from the boredom of the week but to meet at one another's houses at the week-ends and, in a state of half-maudlin tipsiness, kiss one another's wives on the stairs. Even when the average man is sheltered on all sides, weariness, as Pascal says, springs from the depths of his own heart and fills the soul with its poison. Our 'bourgeoisie,' no less than our 'peasantry,' are on the verge of a cultural revolt; they are quarreling with the quality of their civilization.

Now, at the time when a man quarrels with his wife, either one of two interesting things may happen. He may elope with his neighbor's wife for Cuba, fancying for the moment that she is the incarnation of all his unsatisfied desires, the divine Cytherea. Or this man and his old wife may turn over a new leaf and put their relations on a more satisfactory basis.

Which course will be followed depends on the power of self-criticism which the interested persons possess.

This is a parable, with wide possibilities of social application. Our average man, in town and country, is quarreling with his wife, that is to say, with our average American civilization. If he listens to certain counselors who appeal to certain of his instincts and to his romantic imagination, his household, the material civilization which he has slowly built up out of the dust by faithfully working on certain traditional principles—this household will be in danger of disruption. If, on the other hand, his discontent with himself and his human conditions is adequately diagnosed, and if an adequate remedy is accepted, then he will look back upon this period of pessimism as preliminary to the redintegration of the national spirit and its expression in literature. Which course will be followed depends in no small measure upon our power of criticism, which, in its turn, depends upon an adequate point of view.

The elder critics in the academic tradition have in general not dealt sympathetically, or even curiously, with the phenomena. Fixed in an inveterate fidelity to the point of view established by the early classical Americans, they look with a mingling of disdain and abhorrence upon our impious younger world, as upon

a darkling plain
Where ignorant armies clash by night.

The critics, on the other hand, who are endeavoring to deal sympathetically and curiously with the phenomena, are utterly unorganized; are either without standards of judgment, or in a wild state of confusion with regard to their standards. They are making efforts to get together; but they have no principle of integration. I have not time to do more than mention some of their incongruous points of view.

A man whose hearty geniality touches the affections of us all, Mr. William Allen White, proposed the other day, as an integrating principle, the entire abandonment of all standards and a general adoption of the policy of live and let live. His theory of universal sympathy, which he miscalls 'the democratic theory in criticism,' would, if applied, destroy both criticism and democracy.

Our journalistic critics in general, conscious of the incompatibility between their private beliefs and the political and economic interests which they serve, tend at the present time, I should say, to adopt the point of view of universal cynicism.

In order precisely to escape from the troublesome clashes of political, social, and moral judgment, in order to escape, in other words, from the real problem of critical redintegration, another group has adopted the æsthetic point of view, and has made a feeble effort to revive in America, with the aid of the Crocean philosophy, the doctrine of art for art's sake.

I will mention, finally, one other point of view, to which an increasing company of the younger writers are repairing, which we may call for convenience the Freudian point of view. The champions of this point of view attempt a penetrating diagnosis of all the maladies of American civilization, with the assistance of the new psychology. To sum up their findings briefly, they hold that the trouble with American life is, at the root, due to age-long and cankering inhibitions, attributable to our traditional Puritanism. The remedy is a drop to the instinctive level; the opening of the gates to impulse; a free and spontaneous doing as one pleases in all directions.

Popular Freudianism is, perhaps, the most pestilential of all the prevailing winds of doctrine. Yet its champions have penetrated, I believe, nearer to the heart of our difficulty, they are nearer to an adequate point of view and an integrating principle, than any of the other seekers. They at least recognize that the kingdom of disorganization is within the individual breast. The fact that they approach so near to the true destination, and yet fall short of it, renders their counsels peculiarly seductive and peculiarly perilous.

They are right when they attribute the central malady of our civilization to suppressed desires. They are tragically wrong if they believe that this malady is due to the suppression by religion of any specific isolable physical instinct. They are tragically wrong if they think that this malady can be cured by the destruction of religious restraint and the release of any specific isolable physical instinct. When they prescribe, as many of them do with as much daring as they can muster, giving a new and large license, for example, to the sexual impulses; when they prescribe, as if with the countenance of fresh scientific discoveries, the restoration of the grand old liberative force of alcohol; when they flatter any of the more or less disciplined instincts of our animal nature with the promise of happiness in emancipation, they are offering us intoxicants, anodynes, opiates, every one of which has been proved, by the experience of innumerable generations, hopeless even to accomplish any permanent alleviation of the malady which they profess to cure. And when they attack the essential religious principle of Puritanism,—its deep human passion for perfection,—they are seeking to destroy the one principle which can possibly result in the integration of the national life.

Now, as I talk with the members of the beautiful younger generation which comes through my class-room year after year, I find that the Freudians are profoundly mistaken in their analysis of human nature. The deepest craving of these average young men and women is not to be unbound, and released, and to be given a license for a free and spontaneous doing as they please in all directions. They recognize that nature and environment and lax educational discipline have made them beings of sufficiently uncoördinated desires and scattering activities. What they deeply crave is a binding generalization of philosophy, or religion, or morals, which will give direction and purpose, which will give channel and speed, to the languid diffusive drift of their lives. The suppressed desire which causes their unhappiness is a suppressed desire for a good life, for the perfection of their human possibilities. The average unreflective man does not always know that this is, in fact, his malady.   And in the blind hunger and thirst of his unenlightened nature, he reaches out eagerly for opiates and anodynes, which leave him unsatisfied.   But what the innermost law of his being demands, what his human nature craves, is something good and great that he can do with his heart and mind and body.   He craves the active peace of surrender and devotion to something greater than himself.   Surrender to anything less means the degradation and humilitation of his spirit.

This is the tragedy involved in any surrender to subordinate passions or instincts.   I think that our current pessimistic literature indicates that our average man is discovering this fact about his own nature, and that, therefore, like the sinner made conscious of guilt, he is ripe for regeneration; he is ready for the reception of a higher culture than he has yet enjoyed.

Democratic civilization suffereth long, because it is always waiting for the hindmost to catch up with the middle.   It is always reluctant to consign the hindmost to the devil.   But, in the long run, I do not believe that the history of our civilization is going to verify the apprehensions entertained by our old Roman-Americans regarding the average man.   To one whose measure of national accomplishment is not the

rich flowering of a small aristocratic class, but
the salvation of the people, the choices of the
average man in the past do not conclusively
prove the danger of giving him what he wants.
In his first period, he wanted a stable government; and he got it, and wholeheartedly glorified the political and military heroes who gave
it to him. In his second period, he wanted
a rapid and wide diffusion of the material instruments of civilized life; he got them, and
wholeheartedly glorified the industrial heroes
who provided them. In his third period, the
average man is growing almost as scornful of
'wealth and pomp and equipage,' as John
Quincy Adams. The captains of industry are
no longer his heroes; they have communicated
to him what they had of virtue for their hour.
What the average man now wants is the large-
scale production and the wide diffusion of
science, art, music, literature, health, recreation,
manners, human intercourse, happiness—the
best to be had; and he is going to get them and
to glorify wholeheartedly the heroes of culture
who provide them for him.

The great civilizations of the world hitherto
have been integrated in their religion. By religion I mean that which, in the depths of his
heart, a man really believes desirable and

praiseworthy.   A great civilization begins to form when men reach an agreement as to what is desirable and praiseworthy.   The leading Athenians, in their best period, reached such an agreement; and that is why, whether you meditate on their art, their poetry, or their philosophy, whether you gaze at the frieze of the Parthenon, or read a drama of Sophocles, or the prayer of Socrates, you feel yourself in the presence of one and the same formative spirit—one superb stream of energy, superbly controlled by a religious belief that moral and physical symmetry are the most desirable and praiseworthy things in the outer and the inner man.

The prospects for our American civilization depend at present upon our capacity for a sim- ilar religious integration.   Our present task is, primarily, to become clear in our minds as to what is our own formative spirit.   The remedy for our present discontents is indicated by the character of the malady.   The remedy is, first, to help the average man to an understanding of his own nature, so that he may recognize more fully what part the things of the mind and the imagination may play in the satisfaction of his suppressed desires.   It is to help him to recog- nize that even an intellectual and imaginative life will yield him little content unless it is organized around some central principle and animating purpose. It is to give the average man what the literature of our pessimistic democracy has at last proved that he wants, namely, an object to which he can joyfully surrender the full strength of his soul and body.

But this is not the whole of the remedy. It is necessary, at the same time, to persuade the superior men that the gods of the old Roman-American aristocrats have forsaken them, and that the time has come when even they may safely accept the purified religion of democracy. To oppose it now is to oppose the formative spirit of our national life and to doom one's self to sterility. The remedy is, in short, to effect a redintegration of the national will on the basis of a genuinely democratic humanism, recognizing as its central principle the duty of bringing the whole body of the people to the fullest and fairest human life of which they are capable.

The point of view which I advocate is not, as it has been called, moralistic. It is essentially religious. And the religion of an intelligent man is not a principle of repression, any more than it is a principle of release. Religion binds us to old morals and customs so long as they help us towards the attainment of our object;

but it releases from old morals and customs as soon as they impede our progress towards that object. The object gives the standard. Confronted with heirlooms or with innovations, one's first question is, does this, or does it not, tend to assist the entire body of the people toward the best human life of which they are capable? Advance to this point of view, and you leave behind you universal sympathy, universal cynicism, universal æstheticism, and the black bats of the Freudian cave. You grasp again a power of choice which enables you to accept or reject, with something of that lost serenity which Socrates displayed when he rejected escape from prison and accepted the hemlock. You recover something of that high elation which Emerson displayed when he said: 'I am primarily engaged to myself to be a public servant of all the gods, to demonstrate to all men that there is intelligence and good-will at the heart of things, and ever higher and higher leadings.'

IX

LITERATURE AND THE GOVERN-
MENT OF MEN: AN APOLOGY FOR
LETTERS IN THE MIDDLE WEST

Who that sees the meanness of our politics, but inly congratulates Washington that he is long already wrapped in his shroud, and forever safe; that he was laid sweet in his grave, the hope of humanity not yet subjugated in him? Who does not sometimes envy the good and brave, who are no more to suffer from the tumults of the natural world, and await with complacency the speedy term of his own conversation with finite nature? And yet the love that will be annihilated sooner than treacherous, has already made death impossible, and affirms itself no mortal, but a native of the deeps of absolute and inextinguishable being.

EMERSON.

Often, in the repose of my midday, there reaches my ears a confused tintinnabulum *from without. It is the noise of my contemporaries.*

THOREAU.

In eternity there is indeed something true and sublime. But all these times and places and occasions are now and here. God himself culminates in the present moment, and will never be more divine in the lapse of ages.

THOREAU.

*I have heard what the talkers were talking, the talk
of the beginning and the end;
But I do not talk of the beginning or the end.
There was never any more inception than there is now,
Nor any more youth or age than there is now;
And will never be any more perfection than there is now;
Nor any more heaven or hell than there is now.*

WHITMAN.

LITERATURE AND THE GOVERN-MENT OF MEN: AN APOLOGY FOR LETTERS IN THE MIDDLE WEST*

Why apologize for literature at a time when, if we may trust our friends in the eastern provinces who supply us with our weekly reading matter, the entire country is enjoying a literary renascence, and Chicago is its centre? The great industrious city, which one of your own poets has called the "hog-butcher of the world"—this toiling giant has washed his hands of blood and dust, and now in ripe middle age, has turned, we are told, to things of the mind, grants them their full importance, and is become a friend and patron of all the fine arts. This is a very gratifying thought—tinctured only by a grave wonder whether it is true. As I turned over recently the letters of that fine poet and most interesting man, William Vaughn Moody, in whose honor this series of lectures was founded, I could not escape an im-

* The substance of this essay was originally delivered as a lecture on the William Vaughn Moody foundation at the University of Chicago, May 9, 1922.

pression that for him, though he was a native son of our Middle West, his brief sojourn in the city by the inland sea was a restless exile. When he desired to write, he found the air freer in the fishing village of Gloucester. When he hungered for companionship and for recognition, he sought it in the eastern capital. "I feel convinced," he wrote as lately as 1898, "that this [New York] is the place for young Americans who want to do something." On the meridian which runs through Chicago, he felt himself obliged, before he spoke out, to lift the sheer dead weight of a vast busy multitude which attached no importance whatever to what he cared most to say.

Now when an artist is confronted by such a situation, his impulse is to escape; he cannot afford to spend his "bright original strength" in beating against stone walls. For this work, Providence created a lower order of beings, protected by a horny integument from the bruisings of an unsympathetic world: he created the professors and the critics. The first impulse of these creatures when confronted by a hostile situation is to alter the situation. Our Middle-West, in spite of our vaunted literary renascence, is not yet ready to listen very piously to the divine flute-song of "Endymion" or the

"Ode on a Grecian Urn." We think a little already, but not in those terms. Our imagination is beginning to stir; but we are still, as an East Indian visitor lately reminded us, "the flattest-minded people on the face of the earth."

In general, our Middle Western situation fairly represents our national situation. There are little glens of Eden along the eastern coast, there is a narrow strip of Paradise along the western coast, where nature encourages the poetic faculties of men by lavish displays of her own poetic powers. But for thousands of miles between these two oases, through monotonous wildernesses of corn, through wide wastes of grey sage-bush and sand, through ghastly white reaches of salt, one hears only the lowlands murmuring heavily, "In the sweat of thy brow shalt thou eat bread," and the barren deserts replying, "All is vanity and vexation of spirit." Through these deserts and lowlands runs the Lincoln Highway, more popularly known as Main Street. If the pursuit of letters is to be justified to Main Street, it must be justified with reference to a standard that Main Street understands.

That is one-half the problem, but only one-half. If you are going, as the vile phrase is, "to sell" great literature to Main Street, you have got to believe in it yourself. There is the other half of the problem. You have got to believe in literature against the incredulity of your practical neighbours and against the indifference of the world. You have got to believe in it, furthermore, not as a means of escape from Main Street, not as a refuge from your practical neighbours—not this at all. The task is to frame a defense for it which will decisively remove it from the list of the luxuries and the superfluities of life, and which will give it the unquestioned status of bread and butter, plows, rails, chemicals, and gunpowder. And so I intend as far as possible to abandon the high poetic justification of letters, and to attempt establishing their importance by a plain matter-of-fact consideration of their utility. I shall, however, employ the word utility in a somewhat more fundamental sense than that which is ordinarily attached to it, and I shall touch upon certain elementary philosophical matters. Contrary to the opinions of many editors and publishers, this will not be a deterrent to the Main Street mind. There is nothing at the present time which Main Street so hungrily craves as a philosophy.

So far as I know, the philosophers have never discovered any thoroughly satisfactory final object for human activity, except happiness.

The perfect human activity has not yet been discovered. The best that can be said for even the most highly commended pursuits, for the study of science or philosophy or for the practice of beneficence—the best that can be said is, that they are thought useful because they are thought to lead their devotees in the general direction in which happiness has just disappeared over the edge of the horizon.

If I could testify honestly and prove convincingly that the pursuit of letters fills one constantly with pure unalloyed happiness, I should have completed my philosophical justification; and those of you who are bent upon other and competing activities—such as politics, money-making, and marrying—should sell your all and live in a library. I shall avoid the extravagance of testimony so exciting. And yet I think it is part of my duty to say, that the pursuit of letters is in my opinion beyond comparison of all human activities the most delightful. To those who are philosophically minded, this will seem to be the most interesting and important thing that I can say about the subject.

Most people, however, are not minded very philosophically; or rather their philosophy fails to include a frank and courageous consideration of the final object of human endeavor. I think this is a pity. I think our society is the poorer because so few of us make intelligent provision in our lives for happiness or even for pleasure— because so few of us pause to inquire whether our hearts are keeping time with the rhythm of pain or with the alternating rhythm of joy which pulses through the universe. Our dear fellow citizens, indeed, many of them, take a kind of sullen pride in doing without pleasure. Now, the man who does without pleasure himself, rarely gives pleasure to anyone else.

What is still more serious, the man who prides himself on doing without pleasure and on doing without happiness, is likely to listen with a sort of sour disdain and contempt to the claims of an activity which proposes as its end the increase of pleasure, the increase of happiness. I go to him and say: "Let us do what we can to encourage the pursuit of letters; for this pursuit is of all human activities the most delightful." He looks at me with a deep puzzled frown of disapprobation, and says: "Yes, yes, my dear man, no doubt. Delightful, no doubt. Delightful—but of what use is it? Of what practical use is it?"

The sort of man who always asks, "Of what practical use is it?" is called a utilitarian; and our American society abounds in him. The artists hate him and call him a Philistine or a Puritan. The literary theorists of the stricter æsthetic schools do all they can to bring him into derision. In order to confuse and confound him, they have invented a number of oracular and, I think, quite unintelligible phrases or slogans, which they are constantly thrusting into his pachydermatous hide as the *picadero* thrusts his darts into the infuriated bull. I refer to such phrases as "Truth for truth's sake," "Art for art," "Art for art's sake," and "Beauty is its own excuse for being."

If this familiar phrase, art for art's sake, has any meaning at all, it means that art, including literary art, is a form of activity radically different in origin and intention from the political, moral, and other social activities of men, all of which we recognize as having a purpose or end in their effect upon the human spirit. If the phrase means anything, it means that artistic expression is not a vital function of human society at all, but is rather an attractive extraneous thing, a lovely parasite feeding upon the central organism, but related to it only as the mistletoe is related to the oak. Those who contend for this view of art do so, no doubt, with the idea that they are somehow ennobling and elevating art by detaching it from all notions of utility, by stoutly denying that it has any uses.

I think these would-be-friends of art are profoundly mistaken, both in their facts and in their strategy. The wise theorists of literature from the ancient Greeks through the English Renaissance and all the way down to the unwise and bewildered theorists of the twentieth century, have recognized that literary expression is a vital function of society. They have also explained frankly what are its uses. They have not sought to ennoble it by relieving it of service but by making its more splendid service conspicuous. Perceiving that the average man is utilitarian, they have sought to open his mind to literature by widening the scope of his utilitarianism till that enfolding concept contained the uses of the imagination.

The average man, I say, is, in theory, a utilitarian. He is afraid even of such pleasure as he embraces. He is afraid it may not be useful. He will never take seriously to art, to beauty, unless taking to them is presented to him as a duty. One knows the average man. One knows well enough why he attends concerts, visits picture galleries, and, in his student days, reads Ward's *English Poets*. One knows the average club woman. One knows why she reads the authors that she doesn't more than half understand, and why she comes out to look at the poets and novelists, and to hear lectures by the tedious visiting professor. It is not because she *enjoys* it—not that precisely, certainly not that primarily. Why, then? It is because the average man and the average woman have somewhere fixed deeply in their natures an ethical impulse driving them to it, in spite of indifference of the mind, in spite of fatigue of the body. It is because in some fashion they have become infected by our mysteriously potent common culture with the notion that it is their duty, their social responsibility, their object in life, to bring their souls to the fullest development of which they are capable. This is the most promising fact that we have to build on. This is the most firmly established point for the organization of human nature.

The average man is on a pretty safe track, and I wish to confirm him in it. I shall try to justify literature to him as a utility, which is capable of assisting him in the performance of his duties. I shall try to justify it as the most potent force in the government of men, an object which every sensible person is already predisposed to support. But I warn you in advance that I don't mean by the government of men exactly what is meant in the department of political science.

In the committee rooms, where practical men decide how much money it is proper for the State to invest in the various activities of the commonwealth, there is very little said about literature. It is ordinarily assumed that there is not much that *can* be said to the hard-headed type of man about literature. We who are its friends are obliged to admit that it does not directly increase the yield of corn per acre, nor reduce the waste in the consumption of coal, nor prolong the life of steel rails, nor multiply the endurance of reinforced concrete, nor intensify the killing power of chemical gases, nor extend the range of projectiles. The practical man concerns himself with strengthening the sinews of the state. He conceives that agriculture and engineering and business are sinews of the state; and he is right.

But even the most practical of men takes pretty seriously one form of activity which is neither agriculture, engineering, or business; and that form of activity is law-making or legislation. Laws, as he conceives it, are the necessary governors of the sinews of the state. In the degree of importance which he attaches to laws in the government of men and their activities, I think the practical man is wrong. There are six million inhabitants in this state. There is a huge volume of legislation. But I suppose it would be a gross exaggeration to assume that one hundredth part of one per cent of the population is acquainted with a single page of this volume. The laws of the state are a kind of bony excrescence outside the real life of the people. We never hear of a reduction in the tariff or an increase in the school tax but we find by experience the truth in the lines of an eighteenth century poet:

> How small of all that human hearts endure,
> The part that kings or laws can cause or cure.

Such life and coercive power as there are in the laws flow into them from the organism which exists inside the political government, inside the bony excresence of the laws. Society—spontaneously organized by self-enforcing needs and economic pressures and common standards and desires—society generates the power, develops the emotions and virtues which sustain the laws. And society expresses and executes its will, say in ninety-nine per cent of its activities, without formally designated legislators, judges or executives; so that a right-minded member of society has occasion, only two or three times a year, to remember that there are such things as laws in existence.

Society, on the other hand, no member of it ever forgets. For society has infinite functions, and makes itself felt as a formative force upon every member of it on every day of his life. It regulates our intimate personal relations and determines their quality. It gives shape to our hopes and fears, our pleasures and pains and despairs. How does it perform these various, complex and all-decisive activities? How does society get its will accomplished? Well, I might ask those who are so fortunate as to be married, How does one's wife get her will accomplished? Interesting question, to which every one knows the answer. Society gets *its* will accomplished in a similar way—in a somewhat feminine fashion; by lifting its eyebrows, by a disdainful sweep of its skirts, and, above all, by incessantly, tirelessly, day and night, expressing its mind and unpacking its heart in words, till no one fails to understand utterly what it hates and loves and disdains, its enthusiasm and its antipathies, its taboos and sanctions, its penalties and rewards.

We are now prepared for a preliminary definition of our subject: *Literature is the effective voice of the social government.* It is that form of human activity which results from society's speaking its mind and unpacking its heart on all the subjects that concern it, past, present ·and future. The ideal student of letters must, therefore, like Lord Bacon, take all knowledge for his province. The sharp division of the fields of knowledge into departments is an arbitrary and artificial arrangement which exists in universities and in library catalogues but not in the head or heart of man. The modern attempt to distinguish between the field of belles-lettres and the other fields of learning by reference either to the form or to the substance of the productions breaks down at every point.

Shall we make verse the test of belles-lettres? In both ancient and modern times history, politics, science, theology, philosophy, and applied arts and sciences have been seriously treated in verse by writers like Empedocles, Hesiod, Lucretius, Lucan, Milton, Dryden, and Tennyson. Shall we make the subject matter the test of what is not belles-lettres? Many historians, a tolerable number of philosophers, and a few men of science have been eminent men of letters, masters of every art of expression—I am thinking of philosophers like Plato and Bacon, historians like Thucydides and Gibbon, men of science like Pascal and Buffon and Huxley. Literature broadly considered has one subject: the representation of man in his environment. It has one satisfactory form: that which perfectly expresses the subject. It has one final object: the government of men through their ideas and emotions.

Perhaps it may be asked whether what we call the man of letters has any characteristic purpose by which he can be distinguished from what we call "a mere rhetorician" dabbling in history, dabbling in philosophy, dabbling in economics, dabbling in science? Ideally speaking, I should say yes: he aims to grasp a whole which is greater than the sum of the parts. He aims to know the personality, the moving spirit of life, in society. He seeks to know the character of national literature as one knows a person—by a vital imaginative synthesis of diverse phenomena. Consequently his major interest is in those branches of knowledge in which personality predominates; in those expressions of life which are most individual; in those forms of expression which are most clearly marked with the accent and intonation of the human spirit. If this is his point of view, he will be essentially a man of letters whether his field is philosophy, history, or poetry, or whatever else.

The man of letters is studious of the personal and individual elements in literature because he perceives that the social government exists from man to man; and that he who would govern his neighbour must govern him by the stress of spirit upon spirit. It is those men, he sees, that edge the common ideas and feelings of the masses with flame from an enkindled personality who become the chief agents of the social will. "The public," declared Isaac Disraeli, father of the prime minister, "is the creation of the master writers—an axiom as demonstrable as any in Euclid, and a principle as sure in its operations as any in mechanics." The master writers may not in any particular crisis determine the national action taken by the officials in charge of the political government. What they do determine is the national character, which, in the long run, is a far more important object to determine than any particular so-called national act.

In times of critical national action, practical politicians habitually make light of Utopian idealists, doctrinaires, theorists, mere literary men. Any one who occupies himself with the expression of social emotions and sentiments which they regard as inconvenient, they incline to dismiss to limbo as an empty rhetorician.

But as a matter of fact, their contempt for the literary men is transparent bravado, masking a secret fear. The practical politicians have betrayed their real attitude towards literature in every age by exhibitions of apprehensive jealousy towards that formidable rival power which is constantly threatening to take government out of their hands—the rival power of the unofficed individual who, by liberating new ideas and emotions, sets the old government building shaking over their heads.

Wherever the vital part of government is not truly popular and social, the official governors are found attempting to control or to suppress the formation and expression of a public mind. Says the ancient Chinese sage of the Taoist sect, "the difficulty in governing the people [he means by edicts from on high] arises from their having too much knowledge, and therefore he who tries to govern a state by wisdom is a scourge to it, while he who does not try to govern thereby is a blessing." Some two thousand years later, Sir William Berkeley, the Governor of Virginia, a man who seems to have had a Taoist strain in his ancestry, wrote to the English Commissioners of Foreign Plantations: "I thank God there are no free schools nor printing, and I hope we shall not have these

hundred years; for learning has brought disobedience into the world, and printing has di-
vulged them and libels against the best governments. God keep us from both!"

Now God has not kept us from schools and
printing; but politicians frequently have. The
Catholic Inquisition of the Middle Ages, the
burning of Bibles during the Counter Reformation, the Russian censorship under the czars,
the censorship in all the battling nations during
the late war, show us what the practical politician, especially the politician of Taoist ancestry, thinks of printing and literature: "God
keep us from them both." The censorship of
the press is the highest tribute paid to literature
by the practical man. It is his attempt to prevent society from governing itself by the expression of its ideas and emotions.

If, now, we enquire rather particularly why
literature is actually such a formidable power
in the state that Taoist governors ask God to
be delivered from it, we shall be on the track
of the true utility of literature. Aristotle declared, you remember, that literature is an imitation of life. At first blush, there should seem
to be no more innocent and idle occupation than
making, with words, a picture or imitation of
life. Why is an imitation of life more feared

by the Taoist than life itself? The answer to the question involves the essential nature of the literary art.

In the first place, no imitation of life in art is completely reproductive. No novel or poem or history can be anything more than a selective representation. All that it can possibly give us is a reproduction of the impression which life has made upon a particular author. But to select from life is to criticize life. It is to reshape the world in such fashion as to place upon it the stamp of the author's individual point of view.

We talk a good deal of nonsense nowadays about "scientific" history and "realistic" fiction, as if we had learned some new method of presenting a quite depersonalized imitation of reality. And no doubt writers without much character, writers whose souls have no form, can throw handsful of disordered and unrelated facts between the covers of a book without giving to these facts anything but the stamp of a disorderly personality. But the moment an author undertakes to arrange facts in the most elementary way so that they shall have a beginning, a middle, and an end; the moment one undertakes to *compose* a book, so that it shall have proportions, sequence, design—in that

moment he begins to transmit not merely facts
of life but a judgment upon the facts of life.
In that moment he betrays his invincible intention of governing his readers by offering his
eyes for theirs and making their judgment co-
incide with his. For the primary object of all
the arts of expression, is to subject facts to a
design; is by logic, grammar, and rhetoric, to
arrange thoughts, words, sentences, cadences,
accents, and emotional colorings into a comprehensive design of which the final object is
persuasion.

When one studies for the first time Greek and
Roman treatments of education one is surprised
to find what great stress these people placed
upon the arts of expression, upon logic, rhetoric,
and oratory. Cicero, Tactitus, and Quintilian
seem to include all ancient culture, the entire
curriculum of ancient learning, in the training
of the orator; and to regard the orator as the
typical or standard product of the educational
system; as if the whole world for each man were
thenceforth to be divided into two parts, himself, the speaker, and the rest of mankind, his
audience.

What is the significance of that emphasis
upon the arts of expression? Why this, I think,
that they could not conceive of any educated

man who would not desire to express himself; nor could they conceive of any intelligent education which should consist merely in the reception and acquisition of information or of the mere Epicurean enjoyment of the intellect. Every impression should bear fruit in an expression. Every ideal should blossom in an action. Therefore the crown and culmination of learning was speaking or writing with a view to influencing or governing one's fellow men. And that clear purpose, that unifying principle gave to their educational discipline an incentive, a coherence, and a masculine vigor and seriousness, which are altogether too frequently lacking in the lopsided educational programs of our day.

If we aimed, as universities should, at producing complete men; if we aimed, as universities should, at producing the governors of society, we should knit up our literary, historical and scientific studies into an indissoluble bond with the arts of expression, and cease to send out, on the one hand, such shoals of scholars and technical experts who cannot express themselves and, on the other hand, such shoals of scribblers and babblers who have nothing to express.

Every attempt to make an educated man without connecting him with the historical tradition is myopic and absurd; but, on the other hand, all erudition that does not somewhere ultimately come to a focus in the present hour is out of focus; is presbyopic and inefficient.

The ancient Roman writers who thought much more clearly on these questions than most modern writers, drove, even in their histories, frankly at practice. Says Livy: "To the following considerations I wish every one seriously and earnestly to attend: by what kind of men, and by what sort of conduct, in peace and war, the empire has been both acquired and extended: then, as discipline gradually declined, let him follow in his thought the structure of ancient morals—   . . .   until he arrives at the present times, when our vices have attained to such a height of enormity, that we can no longer endure either the burden of them, or the sharpness of the necessary remedies. This is the great advantage to be derived from the study of history."

Says Tacitus: "I deem it to be the chief function of history to rescue merit from oblivion, and to hold up before evil words and evil deeds the terror of the reprobation of posterity." There is the Roman point of view in historical literature. The Roman historian brings his learning to a focus in the present hour; he seeks to govern men by a powerful impression made upon their imaginations.

In the English Renaissance, so largely influenced by Latin literature, the same point of view is adopted by poets and writers of imaginative fiction. When William Caxton, the first English printer, published Sir Thomas Malroy's great collection of Arthurian stories, he announced that he had done so, that noble men might learn and imitate the manners and morals of knighthood. In his *Fairy Queen* Spenser contemplated the fashioning of a gentleman. And Sir Philip Sidney, in his *Apology for Poetry,* following Aristotle, placed poetry above history and philosophy, precisely because of its power to kindle the will to action; because of its superior potency in the formation of character and in leading and drawing us to as high a perfection "as our degenerate souls, made worse by their clay lodgings, can be capable of."

We are now come to a second reason why literature is such a formidable power in the state. The first reason was that literature is a critical and discriminating and persuasive imitation of life, which sets up in the mind of readers a process of comparison frequently unfavorable to the actual order of the world. The second reason is that life itself is, to a far greater extent than we ordinarily recognize, an imitation of literature. The illustrations which come most promptly to remembrance are perhaps life's imitations of religious literature. These come first to remembrance because it is so obvious that the power and the perpetuation of religion depend directly upon the possibility of governing men through their imaginations by inspiring them to imitate some supreme exemplar whose record is literary; so that what is most affecting in the history of ancient Stoicism is the imitation of Plato's Socrates, and the whole history of Christendom, its churches, its institutions, its saints, its sages, and the Holy Roman Empire itself, are imitations, more or less grotesque, of the Old and the New Testaments, just as the moral and spiritual life of Oriental peoples are imitations of the Vedas, and the Koran, and the sayings of Confucius and other eastern wise men.

When we reflect on the imitation of literature by life, we see that there is a third very great reason why literature is so formidable a power. To put the matter in the ordinary way, literature is responsible for calling in allies from the great nations of the dead to intimidate and overawe the living. Governors, still encumbered with the flesh, and the hot-breathed children of the present, who while they strut and fret their little hour upon the stage, like to flatter themselves that the earth is theirs and the fullness thereof—such governors and hot-breathed children like to think that, while they last, they have a right to do with the world what they please and can. Sufficient unto the day, they cry, are the governors thereof; and they bitterly resent what they call the intrusion of the dead hand of the past into to-day's affairs. Now, as a matter of fact, the dead hand of the past never intruded into anybody's affairs. The hands and voices of the past that are felt and heard in to-day's affairs are living hands and voices; are emancipated hands and voices; hands and voices and personalities multiplied and magnified by the reproductive power of the imagination. They belong to the really great society of the world, which is, and always will be, a spiritual society, exempt from the limitations of time and space and death.

To the eager young radical in politics, who is frequently too busy talking to do much thinking and too busy writing for the newspapers to do much reading in the classics, the man of letters frequently seems to exhibit an exasperating and incomprehensible conservatism. The young radical exclaims with heat and indignation:

"Why don't you join us and help us overturn this miserably unsatisfactory society to which we belong?" The man of letters replies, or is frequently disposed to reply:

"My dear sir: We do not belong to that society which you find so miserable and unsatisfactory. We belong to a cosmopolitan society which is as wide as humanity and as old as the world, and infinitely richer and more satisfactory than that composed of those men in the street, who so highly excite your discontent. The trouble with your radical agitation for an international society is that your associates are all men in the street; your cosmopolitanism is merely geographical; your world has no temporal dimensions. You flutter like flies on the window pane; and exclude the larger part of humanity's best hearts and heads. Can you not count on the fingers of your hands all your great men? You are not wise enough to govern the earth."

"Those of the great society, as wise men from Cicero to Ruskin have reminded us, have poets, emperors, priests, philosophers, saints, and sages for their table companions and for the familiars of their peopled solitude—all who for one great virtue or another have merited eternal life. The ideal world in which these presences move seems to our warm youth, eager for sensuous contacts, somewhat cold and insubstantial; but as we advance in age and discover the fickle and transitory character and the emptiness of many of our relationships with those who seem to be living, and, on the other hand, the fidelity and permanence and richness of our relationships with those who seemed to be dead, then the ideal world begins to grow upon us, and its presences appear to our clearer perception to be the objects in our consciousness of the most indisputable reality. Then indeed we know that Socrates and Cicero are with us; St. Paul and Augustine and Aquinas; Petrarch and Machiavelli and Montaigne; Shakespeare, Bacon, Milton, and Bunyan; Descartes and Locke; Voltaire and Rousseau and Burke and Goethe; Franklin and Adams and Lincoln, Emerson, Whitman, and Mark Twain."

"Our association with this company makes our standards of a 'good society' a little exacting. Till you give us better assurance of the splendor of your own projected commonwealth, we shall retain our free citizenship in this ideal community. You will set up in vain a tyranny of shop keepers over this august republic. We shall not be subject to it. We shall obey and follow the commands of the great society, whose members we have known longer, and more intimately, and more profitably than we have known any one of you; for all the great men of letters have infinitely more power today than they had in their bodily life-time; and they retain all the essential and interesting attributes of life. We know their habits and opinions; we hear their voices; we feel their influences; we change our relations to them; we hate and love them; we are intellectually and emotionally begotten and reared and governed by them."

Literature, then, is formidable because it emancipates a man from bondage to the present and makes him a citizen of this state which is as wide as humanity and as old as the world. He may conform outwardly to the government of the men in the street, but his true inward allegiance is to a state which transcends national society, which transcends the international society of the present; and which has no sovereign but God. I have called it a republic; it is more strictly speaking a natural and entirely free aristocracy where no man has any power whatever but the power of his own spirit upon other spirits.

Living habitually in the company of a true spiritual aristocracy has certain decisive effects upon the character. It creates above all a certain internal serenity of an ineffable sweetness. Yet this serenity is not in its essential nature passive but intensely active. It is the serenity of the will bent with steadfast intention upon accomplishing that whereunto it was sent. I have talked with many artists, some in the flesh and many more in the spirit, and have asked them why they chose a career so arduous and so little regarded by the men in the street. And one, an American writer, who but recently joined the company of pure spirits, answered that he had chosen this career because "the cleanness and quietness of it, the independent effort to do something which shall give joy to man long after the howling has died away to the last ghost of an echo—such a vision solicits one in the watches of the night with an almost irresistible force." And when I asked him whether he had been happy in his work and what had been his chief reward, he replied that "he floated in the felicity of it, in the general encouragement of a sense of the perfectly done." His chief reward, he said, smiling with celestial serenity—his chief reward—was "the sense which is the real life of the artist and the absence of which is his death, of having drawn from his intellectual instrument the finest music that nature had hidden in it, of having played it as it should be played."

Now these spirits of the great society are ranked in three orders according to the completeness of their felicity, which is almost the same thing as saying, according to the completeness of their powers of expression, the perfectness with which they have accomplished their will. In the lowest order, are those who have managed only to stammer forth some truth; in the second order are those who have expressed some truth beautifully; and in the third and highest order are those who have expressed a great truth beautifully in speech and act. But not even the spirits in the highest order are utterly satisfied with their achievements. Continually before them, imagination projects an elusive vision of the perfect truth, the perfect beauty, the perfect goodness of which the reality is hidden in the bosom of the All-Perfect. Dreamers like Plato and Augustine represented this vision as an ideal republic and as the city of God. Even the strongly practical, the utilitarian, society of ancient Rome, the masters of the world, felt this teasing, irresistible impulse towards the absolute, recognized this impulse in themselves and deified it in their temples to Fides, Clementia, Concordia, and other types of beneficent impulse—divine projections of human desire and unfulfilled hope.

There is a truth for the imagination in all the myths of religion and in all the fables of the poets. Homer tells us that Ulysses sailed to the limits of the world and poured out the blood of sheep, and up from the darkness of Erebus came clamoring the frustrate ghosts of Teresias and Agamemnon, and the shades of many pale passionate women who had fared tragically in their mortal life. Even so, whenever imagination unseals the gate, there return, clamoring for the light and warmth of mortal life, there return the pale frustrate ghosts of Fides, Clementia, and Concordia clamoring for incarnation. And, with their coming, one feels the rushing current of an impulse, like a mighty wind that has blown from eternity, the impulse of the unappeased human passion for perfection. And when the wind of this impulse strikes upon a man with imagination barbaric and carnal, he burns with a desire to erect palaces, and coliseums, and towering pyramids; and he prophesies like the mad King Herod:

I dreamed last night of a dome of beaten gold
To be a counter-glory to the sun.
There shall the eagle blindly dash himself,

There the first beam shall strike, and there the
    moon
Shall aim all night her argent archery.

. . .

And I will think in gold and dream in silver,
—Imagine in marble and in bronze conceive,
Till it shall dazzle pilgrim nations
And stammering tribes from undiscovered
    lands,
Allure the living God out of the bliss
And all the streaming seraphim from heaven.

But when this breath of inspiration from the
ideal world touches upon a great man of letters,
a poet like Milton or Sophocles, it wakens his
most dangerous and divine faculty; it fills him
with the creative Apollonian madness, with a
clear luminous dream, in which he seems to
himself to behold a law above the law of the
State, above the custom of society, beyond the
practice of the individual man.   His highest
function it is, a truly religious function, to declare the new law.   For this, he is a member of
the great society; for this, he is a free man,
acknowledging no sovereign but God: namely,
that when the call comes, when new light breaks,
when his pulses throb with urgent moral life,
he may rise from the slumbers of his old opinions, and, girding up his loins, lead the faithful

another march through the wilderness toward
the unabiding City of God.

Always the political government lags behind
the customs of society; always the customs of
society lag behind the practise of the foremost
individuals; always the practise of the individual lags behind their private vision and conscience. All the world's bitterest tragedies, its
colossal wars and devastations, the execution of
Socrates, the crucifixion of Christ, the burnings
of saints and sages, the hanging of John Brown,
have been due precisely to this, that the imagination of the world was not yet permeated by the
light which shone through its heretics and
martyrs. That which makes every massacre of
innocents so horrid, that which makes so unbear-
able the destruction of youth and beauty in war,
that which gives to the murderous extinction of
humanity's light-bringers so piercing a pathos,
is that always, in the very hour and place of
destruction, there are meek unprotesting wit-
nesses who know that what is being enacted is a
mistake; there are souls already on the scene,
pure and humane, who pray for a divine inter-
position, and murmur unheeded by the howling
populace, "They know not what they do."

The mission of the man of letters is to be
at the point where, through the brazen dome of

our old habits and customs, breaks the thin
radiance of new truth. His last and highest
function, his divinely dangerous function, committed to him by the great society, is to promul-
gate the new law in despite of the old one, and,
by every power of imaginative representation
at his command, to make it prevail from end to
end of society, and govern in the ideas and
emotions of men. His function, in short, is
precisely that performed by Sophocles in his
Antigone. You will recall that, after the war
against Thebes, Creon, the governor, a precisian and a formalist, ordered the body of
Polyneices, who had made war against the city,
to be left in the fields to be devoured by the
dogs, with penalty of death for disobedience.
Antigone, the sister of Polyneices, one of those
marvellous women of ancient tragedy, who are
vessels incandescent with divine light, recognizes a natural law of kinship and humanity
above the law of the state, and in defiance of
Creon resolves to go out and perform the last
services for the dead.   To her sister who tries to
dissuade her she says:

Do what thou wilt, I go to bury him,
And good it were, in doing this to die.
Loved I shall be with him whom I have loved,
Guilty of holiest crime.

. . .

I know I please the souls I ought to please.

She is captured and brought before Creon for judgment and sentenced to death by starvation. Says Creon:

And thou didst dare to disobey these laws?

She replies:

Yes, for it was not Zeus who gave them forth,
Nor justice dwelling with the Gods below,
Who traced these laws for all the sons of men:
Nor did I dream these edicts strong enough
That thou, a mortal man, shouldst overpass
The unwritten laws of God that know not
    change.

. . .

                              Not through fear
Of any man's resolve was I prepared
Before the Gods to bear the penalty
Of sinning against them.

The Antigone of Sophocles never lived; and yet she lives forever, and preserves about her that atmosphere of sacred awe without which human life becomes flat and unprofitable. Antigone lives forever: and on this fact rests the case for Antigone and Alcestis and Iphigeneia; and for all those proud and gracious figures that sweep along the frieze of the Parthenon; and for all the heroic creations of the poetic mind which fight at humanity's side in the contested passes of history. They never lived; and yet they live more truly than many great ones whose footsteps once left visible imprints on the earth. They live in our hearts and imaginations; and, as truly as Socrates or Lincoln, they augment the power and majesty of that great society in which alone it is worth while to be immortal, in which alone it is desirable to be happy, through which alone it is possible wisely to govern men—because in this society, preserved and in part created by literature, in this alone it is possible to assure victory and reward to those who please the souls they ought to please.